NEWSDAY'S GUIDE TO

Long Island's Natural World

FALCONGUIDE®

GUILFORD, CONNECTICUT
HELENA, MONTANA

AN IMPRINT OF THE GLOBE PEQUOT PRESS

Front cover photos by *Newsday* photographers Bill Davis (screech owl, rabbits, hermit crab, and slider turtle), Ken Spencer (aerial view of Mashomack Preserve), and David L. Pokress (butterfly with flower)

Back cover photos by *Newsday* photographers David L. Pokress (view of Great South Bay), Bill Davis (glossy ibis, yellow warbler, and harbor seals), and Michael E. Ach (mushrooms)

Photo credits on page 134
Maps by Richard Cornett of *Newsday*
Seashells in Chapter 3 are from the collection of Mel Springer of North Bellmore.
Sources for "Trivia of the Tiny" in Chapter 5: Smithsonian Institution, U.S. Census Bureau, International Programs Center, Mississippi State University's Insect Zoo, *Nature*, Ray Lackey, and *Newsday* staff reporting

Text design by Nancy Freeborn

Library of Congress Cataloging-in-Publication Data
Newsday's guide to Long Island's natural world—1st ed.
     p. cm.
  Includes index.
  ISBN 0-7627-3748-4
  1. Natural history—New York (State)—Long Island. I. Title: Guide to Long Island's natural world.
II. Newsday (Melville, N.Y.)

QH105.N4N495 2005
508.747'21—dc22

2004060855

Manufactured in China
First Edition/First Printing

Contents

Introduction

Magic abounds on the island. Harbor seals flop on sun-burnished rocks and then slip into the sea. Carnivorous plants trap tiny insects on the borders of boggy ponds. Creatures barely visible to the naked eye build empires in piles of leaf litter. Red foxes glide through the silence of snow-covered fields, and when the earth warms, spring peepers fill the night with love songs.

And that's just for starters. On this sea-girt world, whose twin forks jut into the Atlantic like the back end of a big fish, opossums bear their young in pouches, baby dragonflies breathe through gills, pygmy forests are forged by fire, and clams buried in sandy bay bottoms extend siphons into the water to nourish themselves. Hummingbirds fly backward and forward and sideways and even upside-down. Deadly plants crowd out native vegetation, and white-tailed deer multiply.

An oyster toadfish, with jaws strong enough to crack open shellfish, found in Peconic Bay

The island is no pristine wilderness or forgotten paradise far beyond the madding crowd. On the contrary, it is a suburban icon—a place where glassed-in conservatories and granite kitchens are the stuff of dreams. Where humans do most of their exploring on crowded highways and in supermarket aisles and multiplex lobbies.

It is called Long Island.

It is almost as if there are two Long Islands. The one that is immediately visible and the other often-hidden world that runs parallel to the split-levels and shopping malls. A natural world of stunning diversity—of salt marshes and hardwood forests, of rivers and bays, and grasslands and pine barrens.

For more than three years, a team of *Newsday* reporters and photographers explored that other world. They waded in bogs, trekked through woodlands, brushed off ticks, and scrambled into canoes and kayaks and cherry pickers and airplanes. They searched for piping plovers and praying mantises and centipedes and cacti. They looked for the perfect picture, the up-close detail. The result was an award-winning series of thirteen monthly sections in the newspaper and a multimedia presentation on *Newsday's* linature.com that took readers into a world many of them were unfamiliar with. Snowy owls and giant turtles and wild orchids came alive in words and photos and ospreys cried out on computer screens. Together, writers and readers explored the corridors of the ocean and the highways of the sky and even dug into the surface of the earth to examine worlds beneath the world.

This information now has been compiled into *Newsday's Guide to Long Island's Natural World.* The book is designed to help readers make their own discoveries in the woods and waters. To help them look up on a busy day and see a red-tailed hawk perched on a parkway pole, or hear a screech owl call on a moonlit night, or wonder at the descendants of a tiny flower whose pink blooms once blanketed the largest plains east of the Mississippi River.

For easy exploring the book is divided into five sections—"In the Sky," "Into the Woods," "The Sea, Sound, and Shore," "The Rivers and Bays," and "In Your Backyard." Each section contains an overview that eases you into the environment, and the *Newsday* team's favorites on the what, where, and when of looking for nature's magic—whether it be chickadees eating out of your hand or "walking" dunes that change shape and location with the winds. Extensive lists offer pertinent details on hundreds of preserves, parks, woods, beaches, and other places where you can find nature close at hand. There are short profiles on Long Island's creatures—from clams to rabbits—and colorful photos by *Newsday's* Bill Davis, whose work testifies to his talent.

We hope you enjoy this book. Davis and lead reporters Joe Haberstroh, Bryn Nelson, Jennifer Smith, and Irene Virag join me in saying, "Welcome to our natural world."

–HARVEY ARONSON, EDITOR

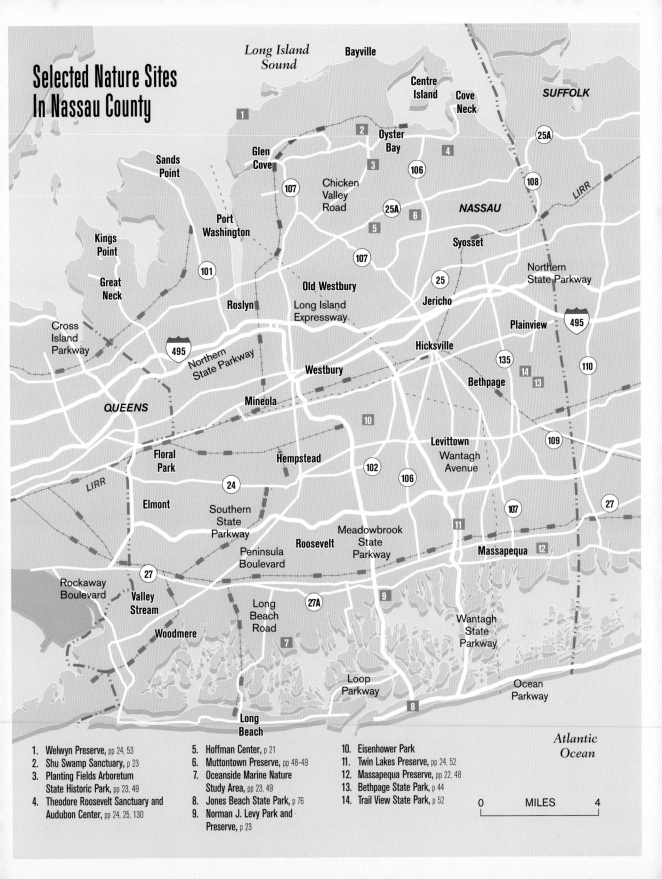

Selected Nature Sites
In Nassau County

Long Island Sound

Bayville

Centre Island

Cove Neck

SUFFOLK

[1]

[2]

Oyster Bay

[4]

[25A]

Glen Cove

[3]

[106]

[108]

LIRR

Sands Point

[107]

Chicken Valley Road

[25A]

NASSAU

[6]

[5]

Port Washington

Syosset

Northern State Parkway

Kings Point

[107]

[25]

Plainview

Great Neck

[101]

Jericho

[495]

Old Westbury

Roslyn

Long Island Expressway

Hicksville

Cross Island Parkway

[135]

[110]

[495]

Northern State Parkway

Westbury

Bethpage

[14]

[13]

QUEENS

Mineola

[10]

[109]

Floral Park

Levittown

Wantagh Avenue

Hempstead

[102]

[106]

LIRR

[24]

Elmont

Southern State Parkway

[107]

[27]

Roosevelt

Meadowbrook State Parkway

[11]

Massapequa

[12]

Peninsula Boulevard

[27]

Rockaway Boulevard

Valley Stream

[9]

Wantagh State Parkway

Woodmere

Long Beach Road

[27A]

[7]

Loop Parkway

Ocean Parkway

[8]

Long Beach

Atlantic Ocean

1. **Welwyn Preserve**, pp 24, 53
2. **Shu Swamp Sanctuary**, p 23
3. **Planting Fields Arboretum State Historic Park**, pp 23, 49
4. **Theodore Roosevelt Sanctuary and Audubon Center**, pp 24, 25, 130
5. **Hoffman Center**, p 21
6. **Muttontown Preserve**, pp 48–49
7. **Oceanside Marine Nature Study Area**, pp 23, 49
8. **Jones Beach State Park**, p 76
9. **Norman J. Levy Park and Preserve**, p 23
10. **Eisenhower Park**
11. **Twin Lakes Preserve**, pp 24, 52
12. **Massapequa Preserve**, pp 22, 48
13. **Bethpage State Park**, p 44
14. **Trail View State Park**, p 52

0   MILES   4

Selected Nature Sites In Western Suffolk County

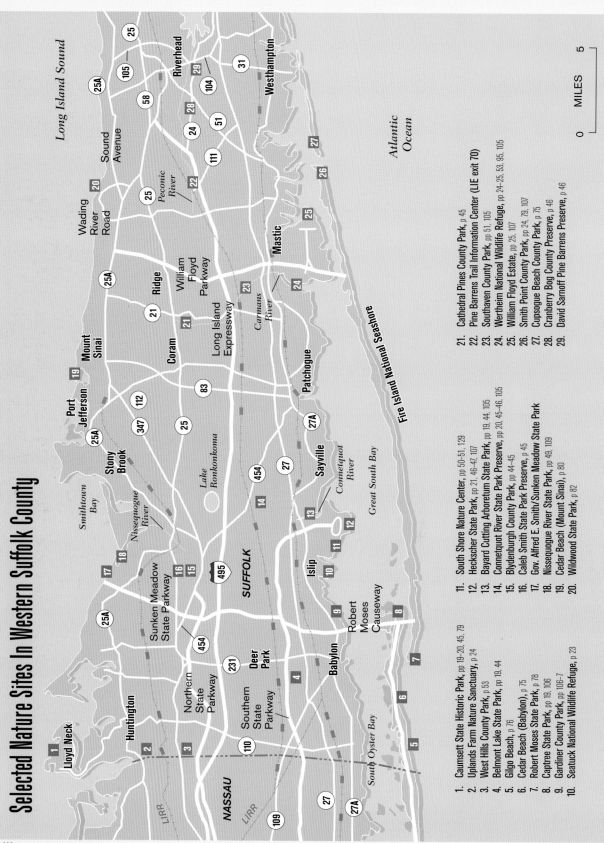

1. Caumsett State Historic Park, pp 19–20, 45, 79
2. Uplands Farm Nature Sanctuary, p 24
3. West Hills County Park, p 53
4. Belmont Lake State Park, pp 19, 44
5. Gilgo Beach, p 76
6. Cedar Beach (Babylon), p 75
7. Robert Moses State Park, p 78
8. Captree State Park, p 19, 106
9. Gardiner County Park, pp 106–7
10. Seatuck National Wildlife Refuge, p 23

11. South Shore Nature Center, pp 50–51, 129
12. Heckscher State Park, pp 21, 46–47, 107
13. Bayard Cutting Arboretum State Park, pp 19, 44, 105
14. Connetquot River State Park Preserve, pp 20, 45–46, 105
15. Blydenburgh County Park, pp 44–45
16. Caleb Smith State Park Preserve, p 45
17. Gov. Alfred E. Smith/Sunken Meadow State Park
18. Nissequogue River State Park, pp 43, 109
19. Cedar Beach (Mount Sinai), p 80
20. Wildwood State Park, p 82

21. Cathedral Pines County Park, p 45
22. Pine Barrens Trail Information Center (LIE exit 70)
23. Southaven County Park, pp 51, 105
24. Wertheim National Wildlife Refuge, pp 24–25, 53, 95, 105
25. William Floyd Estate, pp 25, 107
26. Smith Point County Park, pp 24, 79, 107
27. Cupsogue Beach County Park, p 75
28. Cranberry Bog County Preserve, p 46
29. David Sarnoff Pine Barrens Preserve, p 46

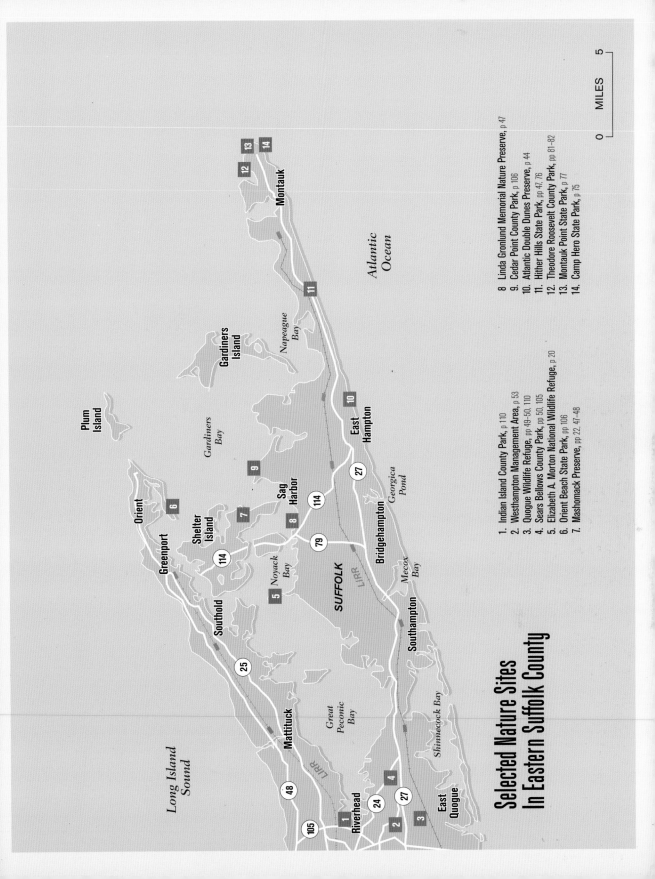

Selected Nature Sites
In Eastern Suffolk County

1. Indian Island County Park, p 110
2. Westhampton Management Area, p 53
3. Quogue Wildlife Refuge, pp 49–50, 110
4. Sears Bellows County Park, pp 50, 105
5. Elizabeth A. Morton National Wildlife Refuge, p 20
6. Orient Beach State Park, pp 106
7. Mashomack Preserve, pp 22, 47–48

8. Linda Gronlund Memorial Nature Preserve, p 47
9. Cedar Point County Park, p 106
10. Atlantic Double Dunes Preserve, p 44
11. Hither Hills State Park, pp 47, 76
12. Theodore Roosevelt County Park, pp 81–82
13. Montauk Point State Park, p 77
14. Camp Hero State Park, p 75

0   MILES   5

CHAPTER 1

A red-tailed hawk over Caleb Smith State Park Preserve in Smithtown

In the Sky

By Irene Virag

They are sojourners from another clime who navigate by the stars and their own inner compasses from thousands of miles away. Many of them fly to Long Island in search of sustenance and to build homes and raise families. Others pass through on their way to more distant territories. Whether they're here for a day or a season, the Island's shores and waterways are brightened by the pure magic of their presence. And the forests that survive amid the suburbs are alive with the sweet and storied sound of their music and the flutter of their wings.

A black-throated green warbler at the Massapequa Preserve

But each and every one of these travelers is just one small part of a greater miracle —the phenomenon of winged migration. A phenomenon that embraces myriad journeys to the place Walt Whitman called Paumanok by more than 300 species of birds from hummingbirds to bald eagles. Tens of thousands of individual birds. Acadian flycatchers and black-throated warblers and rough-legged hawks and ruddy turnstones and rose-breasted grosbeaks and greater yellowlegs. There are more than 9,000 avian species in the world and about half of them migrate. For those that reach its shore, Long Island is either a destination or a pit stop—a vacation home or a hotel. And some birds such as robins and blue jays like the Island so much they live here year-round.

Each of these birds has a story to tell—and some of them are truly incredible. For instance, when the blackpoll warbler leaves its northern breeding area for South America in fall, it has almost doubled in weight to about eleven grams. If it burned gasoline instead of body fat, experts say it would get 720,000 miles to the gallon.

A male ruddy turnstone, left, and a male sanderling near Ponquogue Bridge, west of the Shinnecock Inlet

And forget cheetahs; peregrine falcons are the fastest creatures on Earth, flying at speeds of up to 200 miles an hour at altitudes of 2,000 feet.

Because it is a hub of avian coming and going on the Atlantic flyway, Long Island is a window into the wonder. It helps to have a good pair of binoculars and a bird book, but an adventurous spirit, a lot of curiosity, and even more patience are equally important. You'll find the world of birds closer than you may think.

These amazing creatures are all around us. Look on the tops of light poles along the northernmost stretches of the Sagtikos Parkway and you'll spot red-tailed hawks watching for prey. Plant red cardinal flowers or cannas in your garden and you might just be inviting a hummingbird to stop by for a sip of nectar. Drive along Ocean Parkway to Jones Beach on a clear autumn day or pull into parking field 5 at Robert Moses State Park and you're likely to see American kestrels or merlins or peregrine falcons wheeling in the sky. Walk along Fire Island National Seashore and semipalmated sandpipers and sanderlings will scurry on the edge of the surf. Stroll the trails in Massapequa Preserve or Muttontown Preserve and listen for the warblers or watch for a streak of red that signals the elusive scarlet tanager. Visit Bethpage State Park and in the

A peregrine falcon

woods that skirt the Red Course, you might glimpse the tufted ears of a great horned owl poking out of her nest in a white pine.

Of course, knowing when to look is as important as knowing where to look. The rush of wings swells in spring and fall, not that migrating birds adhere to our definitions of the seasons. On Long Island spring migration actually begins when we're still bundled up in winter jackets. Red-winged blackbirds return in the middle of February, and mourning doves and northern flickers follow soon after to build nests. Belted kingfishers show up as soon as waterways are ice-free. In March woodcocks spiral up and down on the fringes of woodlands in their mating dances and piping plovers whistle across the beaches.

A rose-breasted grosbeak at Jamaica Bay

In April and May wading birds such as glossy ibis and snowy egrets return. And suddenly, it's songbird time—yellow-rumped warblers and blue-headed vireos and black-billed cuckoos and indigo buntings. By early June all the birds that come here to breed have arrived.

Just one month later, the southbound journey of shorebirds kicks off fall migration. In August the warblers are packing up and by Labor Day raptors are on the wing. September brings wintering songbirds like white-throated sparrows and dark-eyed juncos that use Long Island as their Florida. And autumn leaves aren't all that mark October—waterfowl fly in from the north to spend winter on ponds and waterways. In winter the ponds and lakes and bays and harbors are a mecca for ducks—black ducks with orange feet, wood ducks with green heads, and ruddy ducks with white cheeks.

A yellow warbler at Jamaica Bay

A great-horned owl at the Theodore Roosevelt Sanctuary and Audubon Center in Oyster Bay

A merlin at Fire Island

A red-tailed hawk with offspring at Bethpage State Park

As winter wanes, the loons and the grebes molt into their colorful breeding plumage and fly away. The American oystercatcher shows up to feast on mussels and razor clams with its long chisel-shaped red bill. And the red-winged blackbirds are singing again among the wetland reeds.

The cycle of the seasons plays out in the skies above us—all we have to do is look and listen.

American Woodcock

WHAT: A shy, sensitive, odd-looking shorebird that hangs out in wooded thickets and has an unusual courtship flight that is one of the seldom-seen rites of spring.

WHEN: From mid-February to early May, about a half-hour before dawn and dusk, and on moonlit nights. If you stand quietly in a clearing, the plump, pencil-legged bird with marvelous nicknames like timberdoodle and bogsucker, and a long skinny beak and eyes in the back of its head, just might not notice you while he struts his stuff. First comes the mating call—"peent, peent." Then he spirals into the sky, as high as 300 feet, peenting all the way. He twitters and chirps and plunges downward as air rushes through his feathers, producing a whirring sound. And then he does it all over again.

WHERE: It's best to join a guided walk since woodcocks are naturally secretive and their numbers and nesting sites are in decline. Try the Nature Conservancy's David Weld Sanctuary in Nissequogue and the Hoffman Center in Muttontown.

KEEP IN MIND: Be patient and remain still and quiet. Woodcocks spook easily. The male won't do his thing if he's disturbed. With only a six-week courting season, he might not attract a mate, which may cause the bird to abandon the area.

A nesting woodcock

Chickadees

WHAT: Black-capped chickadees. And not just in the bush but in your hand.
WHEN: Year-round, but especially through autumn and winter into March.
WHERE: Not only can you see these tiny birds that nest in tree cavities and are capable of dropping their body temperatures to conserve energy at night, you can feel them alighting on your outstretched hand at the Elizabeth A. Morton National Wildlife Refuge in Jessup's Neck. On a good day you also can attract their cousin, the tufted titmouse, or a white-breasted nuthatch or a ruby-crowned kinglet. The trick is to have seeds in your hand—preferably unsalted black-oiled sunflower seeds. You can see and hear this noisy little songbird that got its name from its fluffy black cap and its melodious call—"chic-a-dee"—along the wooded trails of the David Weld Sanctuary in Nissequogue, Tacka-pusha Preserve in Seaford, Target Rock National Wildlife Refuge on Lloyd Neck, Planting Fields Arboretum in Oyster Bay, and Connetquot River State Park Preserve in Oakdale.

KEEP IN MIND: Don't feed chickadees birdseed mix that contains millet or other seeds, don't offer them bread, and definitely don't give them salted sunflower seeds—salt can be lethal. And don't pile seeds on the ground—stockpiles may draw rats.

A trusting black-capped chickadee at Elizabeth A. Morton National Wildlife Refuge near Sag Harbor

Ospreys

WHAT: *Pandion haliaetus*—the brown-and-white fish hawks that once faced extinction due to pesticides but were saved by a band of Long Island environmentalists. Ospreys weigh two to four pounds but have wingspreads of 5 to 6 feet and plunge feet first into the depths of bays and inlets to catch fish. Ospreys are monogamous, but couples take separate winter vacations, then usually return to the same nest from points south each spring to raise families.

WHEN: They arrive as early as March and leave in late August into September. You can still see some stragglers in October.

WHERE: Look for their giant stick nests that can weigh more than a ton on top of platforms erected by volunteers in wetlands and shore areas from Napeague Harbor to Jamaica Bay. Good locations include Ram Island Causeway and the Nature Conservancy's Mashomack Preserve, both on Shelter Island, and the lagoon at Sunken Meadow State Park in Kings Park.

KEEP IN MIND: Don't approach an active nest—ospreys have been known to dive-bomb intruders. It's not the same as seeing the great birds in person, but you can log on to www.linature.com and watch the comings and goings of an osprey family that nested in the Wertheim National Wildlife Refuge in Shirley. Their daily doings are visible on an "ospreycam" established by the Dennis Puleston Osprey Fund, named for the Long Island naturalist who was instrumental in saving them.

An osprey at the Nissequogue River in Smithtown

Tree Swallows

WHAT: Glossy, iridescent blue-green birds with white cheeks that catch insects on the fly and make their homes in tree cavities and abandoned wood-pecker holes.

WHEN: Their most glorious moment occurs in fall when they migrate south in flocks that can number in the thousands.

WHERE: Perhaps the best way to see these 5-inch-long birds is in early autumn from a boat on the Carmans River as it winds its way from Yaphank to the Great South Bay. If you're lucky, as dusk comes and the setting sun burnishes the river, a cloudlike congregation of tree swallows will appear high in the sky. They seem like a single entity as they perform a curving, swirling ballet. They also can be seen in open areas along the South Shore from Jones Beach to Shinnecock Inlet.

KEEP IN MIND: The performance isn't on Broadway and there's no guarantee that the swallows' corps de ballet will show up, but it's more than worth the try.

A tree swallow at Jamaica Bay

Warblers

WHAT: Colorful little songbirds that are known as the butterflies of the avian world. There are thirty-seven species of warblers that pass through Long Island during spring and fall migration; twenty-one species breed here.

WHEN: You can catch the waves of warblers in spring and fall, but prime time is late April through early May. Pine warblers are among the early birds, showing up in the first half of April to claim woodland breeding territories, while cerulean warblers are among those that show up in late May but fly through to more northerly nesting areas. By September they're all on the wing again in the great seasonal shift called migration.

WHERE: Warblers and other songbirds tend to avoid flying over water, so it's easier to see them in western Long Island. Valley Stream and Hempstead Lake State Parks are good places to glimpse migrating warblers. So are Jamaica Bay, Jones Beach, Sweetbriar Nature Center in Smithtown, Makamah County Nature Preserve in Fort Salonga, and St. John's Pond Preserve in Cold Spring Harbor.

KEEP IN MIND: Migrating warblers and other songbirds move through quickly in spring since love is in the air. Those that nest here — such as yellow, blue-winged, black-and-white, and chestnut-sided warblers — have settled into the treetops of our woodlands by May. Warblers take advantage of tailwinds, so the best time to catch a "warbler wave" is after a high-pressure system passes but before a cold front moves in.

A yellow-rumped warbler at West End Beach

A pine warbler at West End Beach at Jones Beach

Everywhere We Look

BY HUGH McGUINNESS

Ask most people how many birds have been seen on Long Island and the answer is usually between 25 and 75 species. But more than 430 species have been recorded here—and the diversity is astounding.

In a typical year an active birder (the modern term for bird-watcher) can see more than 300 species on Long Island. About 335 species live or visit here regularly and there are about 100 rare visitors.

The rarities are the prizes for several hundred hard-core enthusiasts who regularly cover the Island from Montauk to Jamaica Bay, hoping to add new species to their "life lists," a tally of all the birds they have seen. Birders also keep year lists, county lists, and location lists. One birder keeps a list of birds seen from his sleeping bag.

You don't have to be an expert to become enthusiastic about birds. All that is needed is a field guide, a pair of binoculars, and a desire to identify what you see. Careful observation reveals quite a bit of diversity in almost any backyard. A bird feeder during the cold months and a birdbath during the warmer months attract even more species.

The most commonly seen birds include several species of woodpeckers, mourning dove, American crow, blue jay, the always friendly black-capped chickadee, its close relative tufted titmouse, white-breasted nuthatch, the colorful Northern cardinal, and American goldfinch.

Once bitten by the "bird bug," birders visit different habitats to see more species. The oceanfront provides sea ducks and pelagic birds. Bays and marshes along the shore offer glimpses of herons, sandpipers, ducks, and rails. Old fields contain certain species, such as the grasshopper sparrow and the upland sandpiper, that are only found in grassland habitats. Other species, such as the whippoorwill and the wood thrush, are found only in large tracts of mature woods.

A hairy woodpecker at Shu Swamp Sanctuary in Mill Neck

Long Island is a major wintering ground for certain birds. More than one hundred species can be found in the best birding areas even during the coldest months. The majority of North America's white-winged scoters, a sea duck, winter on the shoals off Montauk. More than 100,000 brant, a small goose, winter in Jamaica and Great South Bays.

A great blue heron on the Carmans River in Shirley

Northbound migration occurs from late February to early June, while southbound migration is from mid-August to early December. During May and September, migrants that winter in the tropics pass through Long Island and the species diversity is astounding. More than 150 species can be seen on a single day—one that begins before 3:00 A.M. to look for owls.

Long Island is best known for its migration "traps," areas where migrants are concentrated. During fall most species migrate at night. When cold fronts are driven through by strong northwest winds, the migrants drift over the ocean. At dawn with their energy reserves running low, the migrants seek the nearest land and fly north to Long Island's South Shore beaches. Once back on land, exhausted and hungry, they are oblivious to the hundreds of birders enjoying the show.

American Robin
(*Turdus migratorius*)

Field Marks: A medium-size land bird familiar to most nonbirders. Grayish black on the back, wings, and tail; darker black on the head and rusty underneath. Not easily mistaken for any other species, although the American robin is quite variable in its appearance, which can cause confusion for beginning birders.

Long Island Status and Occurrence: An abundant migrant and breeding bird. The American robin nests in almost all habitats on Long Island except ocean dunes, marshes, and highly urban areas. Commonly nests in suburbs. Sets up territory by mid-March. Huge flocks can be seen as late as early November, as the American robin is one of our last migrants. Has become a very common winter resident.

Local Habitat: Seen almost everywhere.

Range Away from Long Island: The American robin nests throughout the United States and Canada, except in the Florida peninsula and the southwest United States.

Best Place to See: Outside your window.

Blue Jay
(*Cyanocitta cristata*)

Field Marks: A medium-size, blue land bird and one of our most familiar birds. It travels in noisy flocks of six or more. It is blue on the back, wings, tail, and crested head. Its underneath is grayish white with a dark neck band below the throat. Some nonbirders refer to it as a bluebird, which looks quite different.

Long Island Status and Occurrence: A common permanent resident and common migrant. The blue jay is found year-round in all habitats on Long Island, except in the most urban sections of Brooklyn and Queens. During the fall large flocks of migrating blue jays can be seen along the South Shore, at Montauk, or Jones Beach.

Local Habitat: Found in deciduous forests, pine barrens, suburban areas, and city parks.

Range Away from Long Island: A permanent resident from Newfoundland to southern Florida to western Alberta to central Texas.

Best Place to See: Anywhere.

Common Grackle
(Quiscalus quiscula)

Field Marks: A large, iridescent, yellow-eyed blackbird with a long tail, keeled in flight. The common grackle has two forms distinguished by the color of their iridescent gloss: One is uniformly bronze colored, the other is purplish. Distinguished by its profile and its long, somewhat thick bill.

Long Island Status and Occurrence: A common-to-abundant nester and migrant. Common in winter, especially in agricultural areas, suburban neighborhoods, and city parks. Travels in huge itinerant flocks that roost in marshes. Appears in the last week of February and is gone by the last week of November.

Local Habitat: Found in suburban yards, parks, coastal scrub, old fields, and both coniferous and deciduous wooded areas.

Range Away from Long Island: Nests from eastern Quebec to southern Florida, east Texas to southern Northwest Territories. Winters from Cape Cod to southern Florida, central Ohio and central Nebraska to southeastern New Mexico.

Best Place to see: Almost anywhere.

House Finch
(Carpodacus mexicanus)

Field Marks: A small reddish bird similar to the less common purple finch. The male is red (less frequently orange or yellow) on the eyebrow, throat, breast, and rump, and brown on the crown, nape, back, wings, and tail. Females are grayish brown with a plain, unmarked head, two whitish wing bars, and coarse streaking on the breast.

Long Island Status and Occurrence: A common permanent resident. All house finches on the East Coast originate from illegally obtained birds released by pet dealers on Long Island in the early 1940s. Nesting was documented in Babylon in 1943 and Montauk in 1958. Conjunctivitis spread rapidly in the late 1990s, reducing their numbers here by as much as 40 percent.

Local Habitat: Found mainly in suburban settings, parks, old fields, and other open areas, including the barrier beach.

Range Away from Long Island: Found across the entire continental United States, southern Canada, and Mexico.

Best Place to See: Any park.

Mourning Dove
(Zenaida macroura)

Field Marks: A slender dove with a long tail. The mourning dove has a grayish fawn-colored back and wings (which are marked with six to eight large black spots); a gray crown, nape, and neck; buffy brown underparts; and a long, pointed tail with white-tipped feathers. The feet are pink.

Long Island Status and Occurrence: A very common, year-round nesting resident. Numbers are increased in fall and winter by the arrival of migrants from northern areas.

Local Habitat: Seen in towns, suburbs, farm fields, old fields, woodlots, coastal scrub, and even along the barrier beach.

Range Away from Long Island: Nests throughout the continental United States south to Panama. Also nests in southern Canada. Withdraws from the northern parts of its range in winter.

Best Place to See: Almost anywhere.

Northern Cardinal
(Cardinalis cardinalis)

Field Marks: A fairly well-known, common Long Island bird. The male is our only songbird with a bright red bill and a bright red crest. Females are fawn gray with a red crest, wings, and tail.

Long Island Status and Occurrence: A common to very common permanent resident and nester. The cardinal was regularly found on western Long Island in the nineteenth century. By 1920 it had disappeared from our area, returning in the 1940s. The first nesting was recorded in 1943 at Prospect Park in Brooklyn.

Local Habitat: Found in old fields with scrub and shrubbery, woodlots, suburban yards, parks, and coastal scrub.

Range Away from Long Island: Nests from central Maine to southern Florida and in the west from central South Dakota to southeastern Arizona, also in Mexico, the Yucatán, and northern Belize.

Best Place to See: Any park, scrubby field, or woodlot. Common in New York City parks and Jamaica Bay.

Northern Mockingbird
(Mimus polyglottos)

Field Marks and Similar Species: A prominent, medium-size, long-tailed land bird. The Northern mockingbird is pale gray with two white wing bars on a dark gray wing and a black tail with white outer tail feathers. It mimics songs of other birds, repeating a phrase three to seven times and then abruptly switching to the song of another species.

Long Island Status and Occurrence: A very common permanent resident and nester found across the entire Island. It was very rare at the beginning of the twentieth century, became much more common in the 1950s, and first nested here in 1956 on the Rockaway Peninsula.

Local Habitat: The Northern mockingbird is found in a wide variety of habitats—old and agricultural fields, shrubbery, thickets, suburban yards, urban parks, coastal scrub, and pine barrens.

Range Away from Long Island: Nests from across northern New England to southern Florida and from northern Nevada and southern Mexico.

Best Place to See: Very common at Jamaica Bay, Hempstead Lake State Park, and Jones Beach.

Northern Pintail
(Anas acuta)

Field Marks: One of the dabbling ducks. The male has a coppery brown head, a white stripe along the length of the neck, and a white breast. The rest of the body is gray. Tail feathers are offset by a black undertail and a white flank patch. The bill is a dull gunmetal gray. Females are a warm brown, with a dark gray bill.

Long Island Status and Occurrence: A fairly common migrant and winter visitor, it has bred once on Long Island at Jamaica Bay Refuge in 1962. Birds begin appearing in early September and have headed north by the third week of April.

Local Habitat: Marshy freshwater ponds, in winter, coastal brackish ponds and saltwater bays.

Range Away from Long Island: Nests throughout much of Canada, Alaska, and south into the Great Plains. Winters from Cape Cod to southern Florida and in the West from southern Alaska through Mexico.

Best Place to See: Tobay Pond in Nassau County.

Red-bellied Woodpecker
(Melanerpes carolinus)

Field Marks: A woodpecker with a bright red cap that is often mistaken for the much less common red-headed woodpecker. The adult male has a red forehead, crown, and nape; a cream-colored face, throat, breast, and belly. The back is barred black and white. Females are red only on the nape. Its loud "breep" call is commonly heard.

Long Island Status and Occurrence: A very common permanent resident and breeder. The red-bellied woodpecker was very rare on Long Island until the early 1960s. The first breeding record was from Setauket in 1969. It's unclear why they have expanded northward along the East Coast, but it is now a fairly common permanent resident as far north as northern Massachusetts.

Local Habitat: Mature deciduous forests, woodlots, and suburban areas with tall trees.

Range Away from Long Island: A nonmigratory, permanent resident from Massachusetts south to southern Florida and from southern Ontario to southeastern North Dakota and to eastern Texas.

Best Place to See: Almost any woodlot.

Red-tailed Hawk
(Buteo jamaicensis)

Field Marks: Long Island's most common buteo, adults have a dark-orange tail. They are dark brown above with two poorly defined white circular patches on the back and white below with a belly band of varying intensity formed by dark streaks. Immature birds have a brown, not reddish, tail.

Long Island Status and Occurrence: A very common migrant and winter resident, seen even in suburban areas. As Long Island developed, the red-tailed hawk suffered serious declines as a nester, especially after 1930. Recent recovery of the population may be because of a behavioral adaptation that allows it to nest in proximity to humans and an increase in the number of large oaks, its preferred nesting tree.

Local Habitat: Oak forests for nesting and old fields.

Range Away from Long Island: Nests throughout the United States, Canada, Mexico, and through Central America to Panama. Also found in the West Indies.

Best Place to See: Anywhere spring, fall, or winter.

Red-winged Blackbird

(Agelaius phoeniceus)

Field Marks: One of our most familiar land birds, the red-winged blackbird male is entirely black with a red epaulet (shoulder) edged in yellow. The female is quite different—striped dark brown below and warm brown on the back and head with a light tan eye-line. The female is often thought by novices to be a separate species.

Long Island Status and Occurrence: An abundant migrant and breeder. Fairly common in winter when it travels in flocks of hundreds of birds. Migrants appear in mid to late February and are gone by the end of November.

Local Habitat: Prefers marshes for breeding, but may be found in almost any open or scrub habitat. In winter it prefers agricultural areas, marshes, and bird feeders.

Range Away from Long Island: Nests throughout the continental United States and the southern half of Canada and into Mexico, south to Belize and Guatemala. Winters throughout the continental United States and both coasts of Mexico.

Best Place to See: Almost anywhere.

Snowy Egret

(Egretta thula)

Field Marks: A medium-size, all-white egret, the snowy egret is distinguished from the great egret by its smaller size, a thin black bill, and golden feet on black legs.

Long Island Status and Occurrence: A common migrant and nesting species. Generally arrives in the last week of March and leaves by mid-November. Was almost wiped out locally by the women's hat business around 1900. After protection in 1913 it was not observed breeding on Long Island until 1949 at Oak Beach. Now it's the most common nesting heron on Long Island, with between 700 and 1,200 pairs annually.

Local Habitat: Prefers salt marsh, mud and sand flats, tidal creeks, and beaches on the bays.

Range Away from Long Island: Along the Atlantic Coast it nests from southern Maine to all of Florida and along the Gulf Coast through Texas to Mexico. As a migrant it appears in all eastern states south of the Great Lakes, except in the Appalachian Mountains.

Best Place to See: Any South Shore bay.

–HUGH McGUINNESS

Life of a Hummingbird

They're called nature's little jewels—the tiny iridescent hummingbirds with gossamer wings that beat so fast they actually hum. The ruby-throated hummingbird is the only species that breeds east of the Mississippi River and the only one that visits Long Island. It shows up in our gardens, parks, roadside thickets, and backyard feeders in May and astounds us with its aerodynamics until it heads back to the tropics in late summer.

A female ruby-throated hummingbird in East Norwich

It is the smallest of birds, measuring 3 inches in length and weighing three grams, or one-tenth the weight of a first-class letter. Its nest is the size of an English walnut and its two white eggs are each no bigger than a black-eyed pea. But a hummingbird is a powerful flying machine. Its wings are attached to shoulder joints that can move in all directions and rotate 180 degrees. It can fly backward and forward and sideways—always with its body upright. It can fly up and down and even upside-down. And it can hover almost indefinitely, beating its wings more than sixty times a second while it sucks nectar from a flower.

A hummingbird burns up so much energy that it needs a sugar fix every fifteen minutes. In fact it needs to consume half its weight in carbohydrates—with a little protein in the form of spiders, flies, and other insects—and drink eight times its weight in water every day. Its resting heart rate of 480 beats per minute shoots up to 1,260 when it's feeding. By the way, the hummingbird has the largest heart, relative to size, of any living animal—as much as 2.5 percent of its body weight. At night it lapses into a state of torpor, lowering its body temperature from 108 degrees to about 68 to conserve energy.

Perhaps its most amazing feat is the incredible journey it makes just to get here. Ruby-throated hummingbirds winter in Central America, and in January and February they head north—each little bird all by itself. Within a month the tiny traveler has nearly doubled its weight, storing fat for its journey and is ready to face the Gulf of Mexico. At dusk it takes off, flying nonstop for eighteen to twenty-two hours over 500 miles of open water. Then the hummingbird travels some 20 miles a day, following the blooming flowers northward until it reaches its summer digs in places like Long Island. To attract one of nature's little jewels to your yard, plant tubular red flowers or put out a hummingbird feeder filled with sugar water.

– IRENE VIRAG

WHERE THE BIRDS ARE

By Laura Mann

Birds of many types can be found at parks and waterfronts across Long Island. Here is a sampling of bird-watching areas.

Bayard Cutting Arboretum State Park, three-quarters of a mile off Montauk Highway, Great River; (631) 581–1002; http://nysparks.state.ny.us.

Designed as an estate by Frederick Law Olmstead, this 690-acre park features bountiful wildlife along its five nature trails. Be sure to take the "birdwatcher's walk," a 1.6-mile trail that begins in the formal gardens and loops along the river, where wildfowl come by and an osprey couple are likely to arrive in spring for a summer rental. Best to come during spring and fall migration. Look for chickadees, cardinals, and catbirds.

Belmont Lake State Park, Sylvan Road, Babylon; (631) 667–5055; http://nysparks.state.ny.us.

Stroll along the lake and see American black ducks, Northern

Geese in winter at Belmont Lake State Park

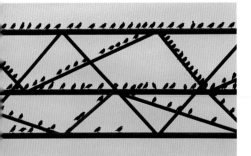

Starlings on a causeway sign support near Captree State Park on Jones Beach Island

shovelers, and mallards. Detours include rambles along two streams and woods, which provide habitats for black-capped chickadees, nuthatches, and several types of woodpeckers.

Brookside Preserve, Brookside Avenue, just north of Sunrise Highway, Freeport; (516) 486–7667.

Enjoy a feeling of isolation in this lesser-known twenty-acre nature sanctuary managed by the South Shore Audubon Society. Millburn Creek flows here. Woodland birds include the red-eyed vireo, tufted titmouse, common flicker, and wood thrush. In the wetlands watch for black-crowned night heron and great blue heron. Guided walks available.

Captree State Park, Robert Moses Causeway, Babylon; (631) 669–0449.

Although the park is designed for fishing, the piers and shoreline provide opportunities to see scaups, buffleheads, and skimmers. Herring gulls and black-backed gulls nest here in April. And check the boat basin for cormorants sitting atop the pilings airing out their wings.

Caumsett State Historic Park, 25 Lloyd Harbor Road, Lloyd Neck; (631) 423–1770; http://nysparks.state.ny.us.

Put on comfortable walking shoes and explore 27 miles of trails in this 1,500-acre park that includes woods, fields, a freshwater pond, salt marsh, and beach. Visitors to the marsh may be rewarded with sightings of green herons, great and snowy egrets, and black-bellied plovers. Look for gray cat-birds, wood thrushes, and great crested flycatchers in the woods. Swallows and warblers frequent the pond, and the beach harbors nesting piping plovers amongst least and common tern colonies. Check the osprey platforms and look for the great fish hawks hunting for food over the pond.

Charles E. Ransom Beach,

Bayville Avenue, Bayville; (516) 624–6160.

The beach is designated as an important bird area by the Audubon Society. You're likely to find horned grebes, Northern harriers, and snow buntings, among others.

Connetquot River State Park Preserve,

Sunrise Highway, Oakdale; (631) 581–1005; http://nys parks.state.ny.us.

Open year-round, the park contains more than 50 miles of trails. There's a chance of seeing wild turkeys, and look for ring-necked pheasants, Canada warblers, and common bobwhites. Watch for ospreys along the river and listen for whippoorwills at evening time.

Elizabeth A. Morton National Wildlife Refuge,

Noyack Road, Noyack; (631) 286–0485; http://morton.fws.gov.

The Morton refuge lures terns among the sandbars through mid-September. Its woodlands con-tain common yellowthroats and yellow warblers among others. And chickadees will eat out of your outstretched hand. As fall approaches sea ducks, water-birds, and sharp-shinned hawks move in.

Fire Island National Seashore,

Fire Island; (631) 289–4810; www.nps.gov/fiis (also see Smith Point County Park and William Floyd Estate).

Fire Island National Seashore is the only national seashore on Long Island. It encompasses almost 6,000 acres of beaches, boardwalks, bogs, and maritime woodlands and thickets. Take a boat or ferry from the mainland to either the Watch Hill or Sailors Haven sections of the island from mid-May to mid-October for camping, hiking, and wilderness trails. Operating hours for the William Floyd Estate and the Fire Island Wilderness Visitor Center near Smith Point County

Eastern bluebirds at Hoffman Center in Muttontown

Park vary by season. These diverse habitats have drawn almost more than 300 species of birds. Migrating birds frequent the area, with warblers in spring and hawks in autumn. Shorebirds include the black-bellied plover, ruddy turnstone, dunlin, and dowitcher. Piping plovers show up occasionally. Woodland birds

A wild turkey at Connetquot River State Park Preserve in Oakdale

include the catbird and towhee. Winter may bring the snowy owl. Unfortunately, ticks enjoy this scenery as much as you will, so be prepared.

Garden City Bird Sanctuary,

Tanners Pond Road, Garden City; (516) 326–1720.

Eighty species, including many songbirds, have been recorded on these nine acres. The site has labeled native plantings and a half-mile of walking trails. In spring and fall look for the golden-crowned kinglet, the American goldfinch, and a variety of warblers. Tree swallows nest here.

Heckscher State Park,

Heckscher Parkway, East Islip; (631) 581–2100; http://nysparks.state.ny.us.

Enjoy 1,700 acres of beach, marshy meadows, and oak and pine woods on the Great South Bay. In summer common and least terns forage on the beach. Look for red-breasted mergansers, buffleheads, and double-crested cormorants on the bay. See the nuthatch, blue-winged warbler, and white-eyed vireo in the woods.

Hoffman Center, 6000 Northern Boulevard, Muttontown; call the Theodore Roosevelt Sanctuary for tours, (516) 922–3200.

Tour this 155-acre preserve for a glimpse of the four to six pairs of bluebirds that nest here each spring. Many bluebirds winter on the Island and flock together to forage; plumage may be even

brighter during spring and summer breeding. The American woodcock male performs his courtship dance from mid-February to May, and the great horned owl can be spotted atop towering evergreens.

Hofstra University Bird Sanctuary, Hofstra University campus, next to the University Club, Garden City; (516) 463–6623.

Featuring a hummingbird garden and a waterfall that filters and recirculates storm water, this two-acre sanctuary attracts mallards, great blue herons, wrens, finches, mockingbirds, cardinals, chickadees, kingfishers, and egrets. Call for guided tours.

Jamaica Bay Wildlife Refuge,

between Howard Beach and Broad Channel in the Gateway National Recreation Area, Queens; (718) 318–4340; www.nps.gov/gate.

In the shadow of Kennedy Airport, this refuge is one of the largest bird sanctuaries in the Northeast and a hub for birds traversing the Atlantic flyway. The refuge encompasses more than 9,000 acres of diverse habitats, including salt marsh, upland field and woods, islands, freshwater, and brackish ponds and bay. More than 300 species of birds have been recorded here. Springtime brings migrating warblers and songbirds. Late summer brings the annual migration of southbound shorebirds. In autumn see migrating hawks, songbirds, warblers, and waterfowl. Species that

Glossy ibis at Jamaica Bay

breed here include common yellowthroats and redstart warblers, ospreys, oystercatchers, willets, and black-crowned and yellow-crowned night herons. Two of the best birding areas are the East and West Ponds. Watch for ticks and poison ivy.

John F. Kennedy Memorial Wildlife Sanctuary, Tobay Beach, east of Jones Beach, Massapequa. Permit needed from Town of Oyster Bay parks department; (516) 797–4110.

The sanctuary lures ducks, both migratory and year-round, and draws owls in winter.

Jones Beach State Park and Zachs Bay, Ocean Parkway, Wantagh; (516) 679–7254; http://nysparks.state.ny.us.

There's good viewing at the eastern end of Jones Beach, where you'll see ducks and migrating shorebirds. The Coast Guard station at the beach draws warblers and hawks through late October. The people's beach is a premier site for observing fall migration, which includes barn and short-eared owls and occasional wintering snowy owls. Take a trail leading from the Theodore Roosevelt Nature Center to the boat basin. A boardwalk will bring you over dunes, where you can spot horned larks, song sparrows, and snow buntings.

Long Beach, on Long Beach Road, off Moriches Road, Nissequogue; (631) 269–1122.

Don't be confused—this Long Beach is on Smithtown Bay, not the South Shore. Enjoy the views where you're likely to find wildfowl such as brant, common goldeneye, and red-breasted merganser. A Smithtown parking permit is required.

Mashomack Preserve, 79 South Ferry Road, Route 114, Shelter Island; (631) 749–1001.

See migratory warblers and shorebirds in spring, and scoters, buffleheads, mallards, and black ducks in winter. Year-round residents include blue herons, great horned owls, chickadees, and woodpeckers. Nesters include bluebirds and piping plovers,

Swans and a flying egret at Massapequa Creek

yellow warblers, Baltimore orioles, and Eastern phoebes. Mashomack is home to a large concentration of ospreys.

Massapequa Preserve, between Merrick Road and Linden Street, Massapequa Park; (516) 571–7443.

Park at the commuter lot east of the Massapequa LIRR station and visit 423 undeveloped acres of woodlands, ponds, lakes, and freshwater wetlands that border Massapequa Creek. Birders should take the bicycle path that follows the stream and winds around the ponds for best viewing. The preserve is an excellent place to see spring and fall migrants. Look for chickadees and woodpeckers. During summer ospreys and common and least terns fish in the ponds.

Mecox Dunes, Dune Road, Water Mill; for information call the Nature Conservancy at (631) 329–7689.

The plant and aquatic life here lure mute swans, herons, egrets, and Canada geese. In late summer when the water level in Mecox Bay is low, exposed mudflats draw migrating shorebirds to feed. Red-winged blackbirds and various species of sparrows nest in the back dune and marsh.

Mill Pond, Route 25A, near Centershore Road, Centerport.

Here you'll see two ponds that rarely freeze in winter. The open water attracts a great amount of waterfowl. Birds spotted here include the hooded merganser, American widgeon and—rarer for Long Island—the Eurasian widgeon.

Muttontown Preserve, Muttontown Lane, East Norwich; (516) 571–8500; www.co.nassau.ny.us/parks.html.

Birding action heats up in May when migrating bluebirds and warblers such as the Northern parula, scarlet tanager, and red-eyed vireo appear near the kettle ponds and wet areas to the south of the nature center. In the fields near the woodlands, see brown thrashers, red-tailed hawks, and Northern bobwhites.

Norman J. Levy Park and Preserve, Merrick Road adjacent to Hempstead Town Sanitation Department, Merrick; (516) 378–4210, ext. 378.

The park contains fifty acres on the former Merrick landfill site. Surrounded by tidal wetlands, the plateau rises 115 feet above sea level. It's now home to wad-

A goldfinch at Planting Fields Arboretum State Historic Park in Oyster Bay

ing birds and waterfowl. You may also spot ospreys. At dusk barn owls hunt their prey throughout the park.

Oceanside Marine Nature Study Area, 500 Slice Drive, Oceanside; (516) 766–1580.

Trek through a tidal marsh in this fifty-two-acre sanctuary, where more than 250 species of birds have been recorded. Uncommon birds spotted here are clapper and Virginia rails, gull-billed and least terns, yellow-crowned night heron, long-billed dowitcher, and Wilson's phalarope. An osprey platform is located south of the pond on the marsh island.

Pine Neck Nature Sanctuary, head of Lots Road, East Quogue; (631) 329–7689.

This sixty-four-acre waterfront estate, managed by the Town of Southampton and the Nature Conservancy, is home to many songbirds and shorebirds. You also may see great horned owls and red-tailed hawks.

Planting Fields Arboretum State Historic Park, Planting Fields Road, Oyster Bay; (516) 922–8600; www.plantingfields.org.

With 409 acres of landscaped grounds, Planting Fields attracts many spring migrants such as cedar waxwings, vireos, and house wrens. In winter you'll see black-capped chickadees, Northern cardinals, and the tufted titmouse. The arboretum is home to a pair of great horned owls.

Robert Moses State Park, Robert Moses Causeway, west end of Fire Island; (631) 669–0470; www.nysparks.state.ny.us.

This park is a common stop for migrating shorebirds. The eastern tip is a draw for hawks, falcons, and warblers. Piping plovers nest here, and summer is a good time to see brown pelicans. During fall you'll spot migrating kestrels and other hawks, and in winter you may see snowy owls.

Seatuck National Wildlife Refuge, 500 St. Marks Lane, Islip; (631) 286–0485; http://seatuck.fws.gov.

The refuge, part of the Long Island National Wildlife Refuge Complex, is bordered by heavily developed areas and is an oasis for more than 210 species of birds. Waterfowl include black ducks, greater scaups, buffleheads, and red-breasted mergansers. Raptors such as red-tailed hawks, merlins, and Northern harriers are common spring and autumn. Ospreys have nested here for more than twenty years. Shorebirds, gulls, and terns show up in great numbers.

Shu Swamp Sanctuary, Frost Mill Road, Mill Neck; (516) 671–0283 (Bob Hornosky).

Spring brings the yellow-bellied sapsucker, Louisiana waterthrush, and the rusty blackbird. Take a walk along the pond's boardwalk for overlooks, where you may see green-winged teals, wood ducks, gadwalls, and buffleheads.

Smith Point County Park, east end of Fire Island National Seashore (accessible by car on the William Floyd Parkway), Shirley; (631) 852–1313; campground, (631) 852–1315; www.suffolkcountyny.gov.

The park's concession stand sits atop a sand dune, and from here you can see scoters, eiders, black skimmers, Northern gannets, and other seabirds. Take a trail from the park into the 7-mile-long Otis Pike Wilderness Area and look for mockingbirds, brown thrashers, and Eastern towhees.

Stony Brook Harbor, Main Street, behind the Hercules Pavilion, Stony Brook.

When the harbor's mudflats are exposed, look for snowy egrets, great egrets, yellow- and black-crowned night herons, and killdeer.

Theodore Roosevelt Sanctuary and Audubon Center, 134 Cove Road, Oyster Bay; (516) 922–3200; http://ny .audubon.org/trsac.htm.

Teddy Roosevelt's family donated this property to the Audubon Society in 1923, and it became the first Audubon songbird sanctuary in the nation. A trailside museum with bird feeders attracts downy woodpeckers, black-capped chickadees, and Northern cardinals in winter. The sanctuary holds weekly programs on bird-watching. Call for hours and programs, including bird walks (registration required).

A double-crested cormorant at Wertheim National Wildlife Refuge in Shirley

Twin Lakes Preserve, Old Mill Road and Park Avenue, Wantagh; (516) 766–1580; www.townof hempstead.org.

Four ponds and an extensive section of wetlands attract the green-winged teal, Northern harrier, glossy ibis, and great blue heron.

Uplands Farm Nature Sanctuary, Lawrence Hill Road, Cold Spring Harbor; (631) 367–3225.

A chipping sparrow at Theodore Roosevelt Sanctuary and Audubon Center in Oyster Bay

Since 1971 Uplands Farm has served as the headquarters for the Long Island chapter of the Nature Conservancy. The ninety-seven-acre sanctuary is composed of open fields, ash and oak hedgerows, vernal pools, and upland woods. In late spring listen to the "dawn chorus" of bluebirds, Eastern towhees, wood thrushes, Eastern kingbirds, and others.

Welwyn Preserve, Crescent Beach Road, Glen Cove; (516) 571–8500.

Watch for shorebirds, nesting ospreys, and great horned owls. Best birding is during spring and fall.

Wertheim National Wildlife Refuge, 300 Smith Road, off Montauk Highway, Shirley; (631) 286–0485; http://wertheim .fws.gov.

With many diverse habitats, the refuge has more than 240 species

Talker, a bald eagle at
Sweetbriar Nature Center
in Smithtown

of birds on 2,400 acres. Birders can see black and wood ducks and ospreys, as well as shorebirds like semipalmated plovers and pectoral sandpipers. Great egrets fly here from as far south as Central America. And if you're in a boat on the Carmans River as the sun starts to fade in late September, look up and you may be lucky enough to catch the ballet of the tree swallows.

William Floyd Estate, 245 Park Drive, Mastic Beach; (631) 399–2030.

Although part of the Fire Island National Seashore, the estate is located on the mainland in Mastic. The grounds are open daily for hiking and wildlife exploration. Look for fall and spring migrants like blue-winged and prairie warblers. The salt marsh that borders Moriches Bay attracts snowy egrets, willets, and great blue herons.

Birds in Captivity

Animal Farm Petting Zoo, 296 Wading River Road, Manorville; (631) 878–1785; www.afpz.org.

The petting zoo is home to the Long Island Zoological Society. The zoo's rescue program takes in abused and unwanted animals, including birds such as parrots, chickens, and ducks, and attempts to rehabilitate and place adoptable animals in homes.

Sweetbriar Nature Center, 62 Eckernkamp Drive, Smithtown; (631) 979–6344; www.sweet briarnc.org.

Sweetbriar is a nonprofit wildlife rehabilitation and education center with fifty-four acres of garden, woodland, field, and wetland habitats on the Nissequogue River. The center provides safe haven for injured eagles, hawks, and owls that cannot be returned to the wild. Seasonal exhibits include a butterfly and moth vivarium.

Theodore Roosevelt Sanctuary and Audubon Center, 134 Cove Road, Oyster Bay; (516) 922–3200.

Promotes conservation and education programs and houses disabled birds such as eagles, falcons, and barn and screech owls that cannot survive in the wild.

Volunteers for Wildlife Hospital and Education Center, Caumsett State Historic Park, 25 Lloyd Harbor Road, Lloyd Neck; (631) 423–0982; www.volunteersfor wildlife.org.

This nonprofit wildlife rehabilitation facility is dedicated to preserving Long Island's wildlife and natural habitats. More than 1,000 injured or displaced wild animals are cared for each year here, most released back into the wild. Several disabled birds, mammals, and reptiles are kept for public education and awareness programs about the special needs of wildlife. Call for schedules.

Bird-watching Clubs

Eastern Long Island Audubon Society, P.O. Box 802, Center Moriches 11934; (631) 325–1237; www.easternlongislandaudubon .homestead.com.

Meets at 7:30 P.M. the first Monday of the month, February to December, at Quogue Wildlife Refuge, Old Country Road, Quogue. The society's nature center—opposite Terrell River County Park, Montauk Highway in Center Moriches—is behind the TWA Flight 800 Memorial;

A mandarin duck in East Hampton

Members of the Great South Bay Audubon Society look for birds at Brookside County Park in Sayville

The Nature Conservancy maintains forty-three visitor preserves open for self-guided tours and bird-watching. For the conservancy's South Fork–Shelter Island Chapter, write P.O. Box 5125, East Hampton 11937, or call (631) 329–7689.

North Fork Audubon Society,
P.O. Box 973, Mattituck 11952; (631) 477–2368.

Meets at 7:30 P.M. the second Tuesday of the month from March to December. Offers guest lectures and fieldwork projects. Call for schedule of monthly weekend walks.

North Shore Audubon Society,
P.O. Box 763, Port Washington 11050; (516) 671–5725; www.nsas.i.am.

Meets at 8:00 P.M. the fourth Tuesday of the month from September to May at Our Savior Lutheran Church, 1901 Northern Boulevard, Manhasset. Offers bird walks 9:30 A.M. to noon Wednesday and Saturday; call for locations.

South Shore Audubon Society,
P.O. Box 31, Freeport 11520; (516) 486–7667; www.ssaudubon.org.

Meets at 7:30 P.M. the second Tuesday of the month from September to May at Freeport Memorial Library, Merrick Road and Ocean Avenue. Offers weekly walks; call for schedule.

open 10:00 A.M. to 4:00 P.M. Wednesday through Sunday, April to October. Walks are usually the first Saturday of the month.

Four Harbors Audubon Society,
P.O. Box 101, St. James 11780; (516) 751–7333; www.home town.aol.com/fourharbors.

Meets at 8:00 P.M. the third Wednesday of the month from September to May at Sweetbriar Nature Center, 62 Eckernkamp Drive, Smithtown. Walks at 8:00 A.M. Saturday from Wild Bird Center, 1320 Stony Brook Road, Stony Brook; (631) 751–7333.

Great South Bay Audubon
Society, P.O. Box 267, Sayville 11782; (631) 563–7716; www.gsbas.com.

Meets at 7:30 P.M. every third Thursday from September to May at Connetquot River State Park Preserve, Oakdale. Weekly and monthly weekend walks September to November.

Huntington Audubon Society,
P.O. Box 735, Huntington 11743; www.huntingtonaudubon.org.

Serves Huntington, Oyster Bay, and Jericho with field trips and annual birdseed sale. Meets the second Tuesday of the month at 7:00 P.M. at the Huntington Library, Main Street.

Nature Conservancy, Long
Island Chapter, 250 Lawrence Hill Road, Cold Spring Harbor; (631) 367–3225; www.nature.org.

An osprey chick about five weeks old in its nest at the Jamaica Bay Wildlife Refuge

CHAPTER 2

Into the Woods

By Irene Virag

Long Island is a place with its own natural history, a onetime wilderness where woolly mammoths and wolves and bears and bobcats roamed, where oak and chestnut and hickory trees crowded virgin forests that stretched for thousands of acres and Atlantic white cedars marched across the swamplands.

Now the great mammals are footprints in the past and Long Island is famous for split-levels and shopping malls and rush-hour traffic. But despite progress and frag-

Dwarf pine cones in the pine barrens near Westhampton Beach

mentation, islands of wooded greenery still remain. A canopy of holly, sassafras, and shadblow grows behind the dunes of Fire Island's Sunken Forest, and stands of century-old white cedars rise as reminders of past glory in Sears Bellows County Park in Hampton Bays and Cranberry Bog County Preserve in Riverhead. And thanks to legislators and preservationists, about 100,000 acres of the original 250,000 acres of the pine barrens still extend across the eastern section of the Island. They sit on the ancient aquifer that contains some of Long Island's purest drinking water, and their ponds and pitch pines are home to buck moths that live to procreate and carnivorous sundews and pitcher plants that lure insects to their deaths.

The woods survive amid suburban sprawl from Hempstead Lake State Park to Montauk Point, and the trees and bushes and the creatures that live among them touch our hearts and our senses.

Fall colors and soaring gulls at the freshwater pond at Caumsett State Historic Park in Lloyd Neck

Haze enveloping dwarf pines in the pine barrens, near Westhampton Beach, with taller trees in the rear

Pink lady's slippers waltz in the wild, and the waxy white stems of a parasitic plant called dead man's fingers that is devoid of chlorophyll and untouched by photosynthesis rise like ghosts from the forest floor. Minute creatures such as mites and millipedes and centipedes and pseudoscorpions fill secret universes in the litter of fallen leaves. Flying squirrels glide from tree to tree, zigzagging to evade predators and searching for nuts to sustain them during winter. The omnivorous opossum—the Island's only marsupial—plays dead at the sight of predators, and at least 20,000 deer roam Long Island, emerging from the forest to invade farms and backyards from the East End to Lloyd Neck.

The forests are sanctuaries from the hurry and hustle of stores and offices. They are for walking and watching. Some are far from developed areas while others are refuges where the sights and scents and the sounds of silence border the very edge of parkways and highways.

A twelve-week old flying squirrel found in Seaford

An aerial view of the inlet and wetlands of Shelter Island's Mashomack Preserve

At far-flung Mashomack Preserve on Shelter Island—a pristine 2,000-acre sanctuary with 22 miles of marked hiking trails—visitors can imagine the way Long Island must have been when the Manhanset Indians strode through the forest in search of game or gazed across the water to Gardiners Island and Plum Island. Muskrats, foxes, and deer live in the tangled woods that open to vistas of bays and inlets, and terrapins and glossy ibis go about their days. Sometimes, visiting eagles and river otter stop by.

A juvenile bald eagle on a February day at Connetquot River State Park Preserve

A deer and Canada geese at Connetquot River State Park Preserve

On the other hand a walker on the trail at Connetquot River State Park Preserve in Oakdale may well spot deer gathered in a clearing beneath tall pitch pines not far from Sunrise Highway. And along the path she can stop to scratch the bark of spicebush and inhale its sweet smell. At Caleb Smith State Park Preserve in Smithtown, night hikers in search of bats and other nocturnal creatures can see car lights along Jericho Turnpike through the trees. There are, incidentally, seven species of bats that inherit the night on Long Island. None feed on blood and their diet is in fact beneficial to humans: One little brown bat can eat 6,000 mosquitoes in a single night.

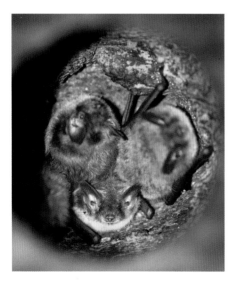

Everywhere on Long Island, nature beckons. Stick to the path, and no place is more welcoming than the woods.

Bats, creatures of the night, roosting in a barn rafter at Blydenburgh County Park in Smithtown

Atlantic White Cedars

What: Before the settlers came the East End was patched with swampland dominated by tightly packed Atlantic white cedars that grew 60 to 89 feet high. Now only a few good stands of the old cedars remain.

When: Winter is best, because birds seek shelter in the evergreen cedars. Once spring comes to the Island, birds are more likely to visit deciduous trees.

Where: On the borders of Sears Pond and Bellows Pond in Sears Bellows County Park, Bellows Pond Road in Flanders, (631) 852–8290; Cranberry Bog County Preserve, Riverhead Moriches Road in Riverhead, (631) 854–4949; Blydenburgh County Park, Veterans Memorial Highway in Smithtown, (631) 854–3713; Gardiner County Park, Montauk Highway in West Bay Shore, (631) 854–0935; and Tackapausha County Preserve, Washington Avenue in Seaford, (516) 571–7443.

Keep in Mind: Wear boots or hip waders. White cedars grow in shallow swamps—generally too shallow for fish but not for walkers—so naturalists advise visitors to take great care not to trip while slogging through the stands of old trees.

A tall Atlantic white cedar at Blydenburgh County Park in Smithtown

Carnivorous plants

What: Sundews, bladderworts, and pitcher plants. What these bog-loving plants have in common is that they're all insect-eating carnivores. Pitcher plants use nectar to entice insects, which tumble off their leaves into the plant's pool of rainwater and digestive juices. Sundews secrete a gooey substance to catch their dinners. And the leaves of bladderworts have tiny trapdoors that open when something appetizing floats by.

When: Pitcher plants are around all year but are best seen when they flower in spring. Sundews and bladderworts bloom in early to mid-July.

Where: Look for pitcher plants with their 8-inch pitcher-shaped leaves along the boardwalk at the Quogue Wildlife Refuge on Old Country Road in Quogue. Call (631) 653–4771; www .quoguerefuge.com. A good spot for sundews and bladderworts is the Calverton Ponds Preserve on Old River Road in Calverton; call (631) 367–3225 or go to www.nature.org/longisland. These tiny plants live in shallow water along the edges of the ponds. Sundews come in three varieties: round-leafed, spatulate-leafed, and thread-leaved. There are a half dozen species of bladderworts that are native to the Island—one has purple blooms, the others flower in yellow.

Keep in Mind: Don't try to pick these plants—they won't eat you, but they only grow where nature intended them to. They will not grow in your garden. And don't step on them; they're very fragile.

An insect-trapping pitcher plant in Quogue

The Fairhaven Beech

What: Although it does not grow in a forest, the great copper beech of Planting Fields Arboretum in Oyster Bay is one of Long Island's most famous and impressive trees. Officially known as the Fairhaven Beech, the majestic tree is more than 60 feet tall with a spread of almost a quarter acre. It is a metaphor for the way trees branch through our hearts and our lives and our landscapes. In 1915 when the beech was threatened with destruction, insurance magnate William Robertson Coe had it transported by land and sea from the childhood home of his wife, Mai Rogers Coe, in Fairhaven, Massachusetts, to their estate in Oyster Bay.

When: Throughout the year, but especially in April when the leaves unfurl and the tree shimmers with a coppery tinge in the sunlight.

Where: Planting Fields Arboretum State Historic Park, Planting Fields Road, Oyster Bay. The copper beech reigns outside Coe Hall. Call (516) 922–8600; www.plantingfields.com.

Keep in Mind: Stay outside the fence. The copper beech's days are numbered and, despite its size, the tree is fragile. And while you're there, take advantage of the arboretum gardens, woodland paths, and exhibits.

The famous Fairhaven Beech at Planting Fields Arboretum State Historic Park in Oyster Bay

The Pine Barrens

An egret gliding above Hubbard County Park in Flanders

What: The pine barrens is one of Long Island's greatest natural treasures. Its soil bed is porous, acidic, and nutrient poor, allowing rainwater to drain through to the Island's largest underground aquifer. Crops wither in these desertlike conditions, but the pines survive with little water. The forest has weathered a millennia of fires that burned away other trees, leaving dwarf pines that stand just 5 or 6 feet tall, and pitch pines that reach more than 100 feet and form a cathedral of branches shading the forest's floor. The barrens are a mosaic of mossy bogs, salt marshes, willowy creeks, and hillsides with berry bushes. Inhabitants include deer, box turtles, hognose snakes, red foxes, opossums and warblers. Wild orchids and small carnivorous plants live in the barrens as well.

When: Anytime, but access is best in summer.

Where: The forest covers 100,000 acres in the towns of Brookhaven, Southampton, and Riverhead. Since it embraces private, county, and state land, it's a good idea to get a map and hiking advice from the Long Island Greenbelt Trail Conference at (631) 360–0753. Another good place to check out hiking trails in the barrens and other locales is www.hike-li.org. Access to state-owned land in the forest requires a free permit. Call the New York State Department of Environmental Conservation at (631) 444–0273 for an application and details. Hiking or bird-watching at some Suffolk County sites requires a Green Key access card; call (631) 854–4949. Nature guides and trail maps are available at Pine Barrens Trail Information Center in Manorville, off exit 70 of the Long Island Expressway. The office is staffed from April to October, Friday through Monday; (631) 369–9768.

Keep in Mind: The pine barrens is a fragile ecosystem that is being blighted by all-terrain vehicles and garbage. Remember to leave this unique place as you found it. Take only photographs and leave only footprints.

The colorful pine barrens, south of Riverhead, on a November day

The Woods at Night

What: Long Island's darkened woodlands offer a unique vantage on the nocturnal world, where touches and sounds often vie with sights for supremacy. Brown bats frequent the night skies of summer, while screech owls and great horned owls often rule winter nights. Well-trained ears can sometimes pick out the high-pitched squeaks of Southern flying squirrels in the trees overhead, while patient eyes can occasionally make out the tracks or shapes of opossums, raccoons, and red foxes below.

When: Anytime, though animals are often less active during a full moon.

Where: Seasonal night hikes are offered by the Sweetbriar Nature Center, 62 Eckernkamp Drive in Smithtown, (631) 979–6344; the Theodore Roosevelt Sanctuary and Audubon Center, 134 Cove Road in Oyster Bay, (516) 922–3200; and the Seatuck Environmental Association in Islip, (631) 581–6908. Eric Powers, an outdoor education specialist based at Caleb Smith State Park Preserve in Smithtown, guides many of these hikes. Powers runs a nature awareness company called Your Connection to Nature, which also offers night outings. For times and fees call (631) 241–0088.

Keep in Mind: Suburban folklore suggests that a screech owl or great horned owl lives in every neighborhood, so keep your eyes—and ears—open.

Raccoons in an old tree in Stony Brook

American Elm
(Ulmus americana)

The American elm reaches 40 to 60 feet tall, and its branches begin forking 20 to 40 feet from the ground. It has grayish, furrowed bark, and clusters of papery tan flowers that are both male and female and bloom two to three weeks in early spring. Its leaves have the shape of two hands cupped together in prayer and are 2 to 5 inches long. Trees begin producing seeds when they reach about forty years old. American elms reach 175 to 200 years old.

American Sycamore
(Platanus occidentalis)

This massive tree has heavy branches and a maze of zigzagging twigs. The thin bark flakes off, leaving patches of brown, white, and green. The leaves have three to five lobes, each with a rim of teeth. They unfold in white clusters. The spherical fruit hangs from a 3- to 6-inch stalk. The fruit's "fur" attaches to seeds, so the seeds can take flight in the late fall winds. Trees more than one-hundred years old are often hollow inside and become homes to ducks, opossums and raccoons. American sycamores, also called Eastern sycamores, can grow to 120 feet tall.

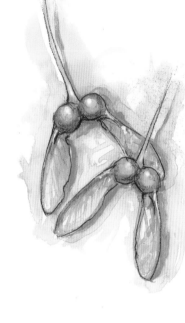

Pitch Pine

(Pinus rigida)

The pitch pine, with stiff needles and red-brown, furrowed bark, can reach 20 to 100 feet tall. The 4- to 5-inch needles are clustered in bundles of three, unlike most other pines that have needle bundles of two. The needles last two years. The pitch pine's red-yellow flowers bloom in April and May. Trees begin producing egg-shaped cones at eight to ten years old, and live for 200 years. Cones sometimes cling to trees for ten to twelve years before falling.

Red Maple

(Acer rubrum)

This tree, which grows 30 to 90 feet, is usually the first to flower in spring. Clusters of red buds hang from drooping 2-inch stalks, blanketing fields in red. The leaves—with their triangular lobes and small teeth—unfold a bright red and turn green as they mature. A red maple produces 12,000 to 91,000 seeds annually, and the winged fruit comes in red, green, and yellow. Red maples reach 80 to 150 years old.

Sassafras

(Sassafras albidum)

The sassafras has just a few large branches that shoot up, each with a full bouquet of leaf-filled smaller branches at their tips. The tree's fruit is small balls of blue on red stalks, and its flowers are green-yellow. The sassafras's leaves come in different shapes—some elliptical, some oval—and they have one, two, or three lobes. The leaves can grow to 6 inches and turn red and yellow in fall. When broken, the twigs have a sweet, spicy smell like root beer. The outer bark is coarse, with large ridges. The inner bark has a rich, cinnamon color. The tree grows from 10 to 50 feet. Except in moist areas, sassafras trees rarely live longer than thirty years.

Sweetgum

(Liquidambar styraciflua)

The sweetgum is known for its varied and long fall foliage and its star-shaped leaves that have a sweet fragrance when crushed. Its prickly, round fruit hangs from short stalks. The trees produce an abundance of seeds until they reach about 150 years old, with each fruit carrying up to fifty seeds. The fruit becomes ripe from September to November. The flowers are small and green, and the bark gray-brown with irregular ridges. The crowns are rounded on young trees and spread out on older ones. Sweetgums grow from 50 to 150 feet tall.

Yellow Poplar or Tuliptree

(Liriodendron tulipifera)

Yellow poplars can soar to 200 feet, and from April to June produce thousands of cup-like green-yellow flowers that hide in the leaves. When a yellow poplar reaches about fifteen years of age, it produces cone-shaped fruits that fall from October to November, when the tree's leaves have turned yellow. Roughly 65 percent of the sun-loving tree's trunk is free of branches, and its bark is light gray with thin grooves. It can live as long as 500 years.

White Pine

(Pinus strobus)

The tall white pine, which grows from 80 to 100 feet, is a magnificent evergreen. The tree's trunk is very straight and grows quickly— 60 feet in its first forty years. The crown is conical in its early years and becomes wispier as the tree grows older. The white pine is the only pine east of the Rockies whose needles come in bunches of five. The needles are slim and flexible and 2 to 4 inches long. Yellow and green flowers form tight bunches at the end of branches. The branches are covered in deeply ridged bark. White pines usually reach 250 years old.

–JULIE CLAIRE DIOP

Life of an Opossum

With the heft of a house cat but the intelligence of a dog, the tail of a rat but the pouch of a kangaroo, and a survival strategy that includes munching on roadkill and then mimicking it, the Virginia opossum is something of a walking contradiction.

Originally called "apasum," an Algonquian word that means "white animal," the furry mammal with the pointed snout and leathery ears received its current name after European colonists first saw the nocturnal creature in the colony of Virginia in the early 1600s. Present-day admirers sometimes call Long Island's lone marsupial "nature's little sanitation engineer," a euphemistic reference to its indiscriminate palate.

Although its North American heritage stretches back more than seventy million years, scientists believe that *Didelphis virginiana* became established on Long Island only in the late 1800s, perhaps due to accidental releases of the traditional southern species by settlers.

Frequently frostbitten ears and tail notwithstanding, the opossum found the Island much to its liking and multiplied. Farmers were not pleased with this proliferation, and by the late 1880s several Long Island towns had begun paying bounties for dead opossums.

Although the nuisance label has faded with time, the omnivorous animal still lives and travels near humans, whether along the boardwalk on the Rockaway peninsula, by a busy office complex in Melville, or near a North Fork byway. But recurrent trash bin diving and garden pillaging are unlikely to involve the same opossum, since the nomadic animal seldom stays put for very long.

Born less than two weeks after their parents mate, the honeybee-size opossum young must follow a moistened trail from the mother's birth canal to reach her fur-lined pouch. The survivors remain within the pouch for two months, where they develop while sucking milk from the mother's teats. Eventually, the mother coaxes her youngsters onto her back, where they stay for another month or so. When the fully weaned opossums fall off, they are often left to fend for themselves.

Fortunately, an opossum is blessed with a set of well-developed survival skills, not the least of which is its wide-ranging diet. With opposable thumbs on its hind feet, the animal can readily climb trees, whether for lodging or safety, and its prehensile tail offers leverage and aids in carrying bedding material.

The opossum also has more teeth than any other North American land mammal and will bare many of its fifty pearly whites when threatened. The display is largely theatrical, however, and intense fear triggers the animal's best-known defense mechanism, commonly called "playing 'possum." To ward off an attack by a predator such as a dog or red fox, the opossum rolls over, closes its eyes, and feigns death—a strategy apparently designed to dissuade attackers hoping for a more animated chase.

—BRYN NELSON

An opossum used for educational programs at Caumsett State Historic Park in Lloyd Neck

ON THE TRAILS

By Laura Mann

Here are dozens of unspoiled areas open to the public. Call ahead if a listing cites a need for a special permit.

Andy Warhol Visual Arts Preserve, Route 27 east, 2 miles past Montauk Village; (631) 329–7689; www.nature.org.

This Nature Conservancy property preserves the Montauk Moorlands. In maritime tall shrub lands and forests, trees here include shadbush, American holly, sassafras, red maple, and black oak. Toward the water, trees grow shorter due to the effects of the saltwater breeze. Closest to the ocean are bayberry, highbush blueberry, and sweet pepperbush. Rare animals include the Eastern newt, spotted turtle, blue-spotted salamander, Eastern hognose snake, and bog copper butterfly. Visitors welcome by appointment. The site hosts at least four arts programs a year.

Atlantic Double Dunes, Atlantic Avenue to Old Beach Lane, Amagansett; (631) 329–7689; www.nature.org.

Call the Nature Conservancy during summer for a guided tour of this three-acre preserve. It has primary and secondary dunes, a freshwater marsh, and a maritime oak forest. The secondary dune is home to oak, shadbush, and pitch pine. Look for deer, red fox, and box turtles. Also look for rare orchids and the Eastern spadefoot toad.

Turtles basking at Caleb Smith State Park Preserve in Smithtown

Bailey Arboretum, Bayville Road and Feeks Lane, Lattingtown; (516) 571–8020; www.co.nassau .ny.us/parks.html.

Has forty-two acres, self-guided nature trails. Exceptional collection of conifers. Daffodils in April, flowering trees in spring, annuals and perennials throughout summer. Sensory garden for the disabled.

Bayard Cutting Arboretum State Park, exit 45E (Montauk Highway), east three-quarters of a mile to arboretum, Great River; (631) 581–1002; http://nysparks .state.ny.us.

Five nature walks explore 690 acres in an idyllic setting along the Connetquot River. Giant tulip trees, oaks, and maples— many more than one hundred years old—grow near the larger pond. Exotic species include the dwarf nikko, blue atlas cedar, and dawn redwood.

Belmont Lake State Park, Southern State Parkway, exit 38, North Babylon; (631) 667–5055; http://nysparks.state.ny.us.

This 459-acre park surrounds a lovely lake, with picnic and play areas, 2 miles of biking and walking trails, bridle path with rentals, rowboat rentals, and freshwater fishing (with license).

Bethpage State Park, 99 Quaker Meetinghouse Road, Farmingdale; (516) 249–0701; http://nysparks.state.ny.us.

This park is famous for its golf courses but also offers a 5-mile stretch of the Nassau–Suffolk Trail, with views of small animals and native plants; call (631) 360–0753 for trail tours.

Blydenburgh County Park, Veterans Memorial Highway, Smithtown; (631) 854–3713; www.suffolkcountyny.gov.

Features 588 acres with bridle paths, campsites, freshwater fishing, hiking trails, picnic areas, and rowboat rentals.

Brookside Preserve, Brookside Avenue, just north of Sunrise Highway, Freeport; (516) 486–7667.

This twenty-acre preserve managed by the South Shore Audubon Society holds red maple, red oak, sassafras, beech, tupelo, cherry, and white oak. The large leaves of the umbrella magnolia and the lesser celandine's carpet of yellow flowers are highlights. Guided tours are available by calling the Audubon Society at (516) 486–7667.

Caleb Smith State Park Preserve, off Jericho Turnpike, a half-mile east of Old Willets Pass, Smithtown; (631) 265–1054; http://nysparks.state.ny.us.

Pick up a free tree guide in the park office before starting one of the self-guided trails at this 543-acre preserve. Wineberry and raspberry bushes, wild grapes and wild roses, and oaks, locust, and black cherry trees grow along the

A bullfrog at Caleb Smith State Park Preserve in Smithtown

trails. Deep into the woods are Canada mayflower, nodding trillium, and turk's-cap lily. Poison ivy is common. Mice, voles, shrews, and moles live here. The freshwater section of the Nissequogue River flows through, and skunk cabbage, red maples, and spicebush grow near the river. In spring wet areas become vernal ponds where tree frogs, salamanders, and spring peepers breed.

Calverton Ponds Preserve, Wading River Manor Road to Old River Road, Calverton; (631) 367–3225; www.nature.org.

These 350 acres in the Long Island pine barrens are managed by the Nature Conservancy and Suffolk County. The site contains one of the highest concentrations of rare and endangered plants and animals in New York State. Pitch pine, oak trees, a shrub layer of scrub oak, huckleberry, and blueberry grow. Look for the rare tiger salamander or the banded sunfish in the ponds.

Cathedral Pines County Park, Yaphank–Middle Island Road, Middle Island; (631) 852–5500; www.suffolkcountyny.gov.

On 320 acres are campsites, restrooms, bridle paths, and 3 miles of nature trails.

Caumsett State Historic Park, 25 Lloyd Harbor Road, Lloyd Neck; (631) 423–1770; http://nysparks.state.ny.us.

The park has 27 miles of trails and some 1,500 acres of woodlands, meadows, shoreline, salt marsh,

Hiking through the 350-acre Calverton Ponds Preserve, home to many rare plants and animals

and gardens. The hardwood forest includes red, white, and black oak; black birch; flowering dogwood; sassafras; and witch hazel. The park is home to the Volunteers for Wildlife Hospital and Education Center (see page 55).

Connetquot River State Park Preserve, north side of Sunrise Highway, just west of Pond Road, Oakdale; (631) 581–1005; http://nysparks.state.ny.us.

Access to the preserve is by free permit only, available by writing to P.O. Box 505, Oakdale 11769. The park offers more than 50 miles of hiking trails and bridle paths on 3,473 acres. The Connetquot River is a favorite spot for fishing. Pitch pine and oak line the river and nearby woods. While most of the park's woods are 20 to 40 feet tall, about 200 acres is composed of dwarf oak brush and pine barrens. Look for deer, raccoons, chipmunks, and bats.

Cow Meadow Park Preserve,
foot of South Main Street, Freeport; (516) 571–8685; www.co.nassau.ny.us/parkmuse .html.

On the southern tip of the Freeport peninsula, this Nassau County preserve offers 150 acres of saltwater marsh and estuary creeks. Two nature trails take you through maritime thicket composed mainly of silverberry, Asiatic bittersweet, edible sumac, crabapple, hawthorn, and beach rose. Tidal marshes are covered with phragmites and spartina. Look for fiddler crabs along the tidal channels.

Cranberry Bog County Preserve,
Riverhead Moriches Road, 1 mile south of traffic circle, Riverhead; (631) 854–4949.

Has 460 acres in pine barrens, with wetlands and woodlands, and a three-quarter-mile interpretive trail around Sweezy Pond. Group activities by permit.

David Sarnoff Pine Barrens Preserve,
Route 104, Riverhead; (631) 444–0273; www.dec.state .ny.us.

Open year-round, except in January deer-hunting season. Access by New York State Department of

Environmental Conservation permit (free). Features 2,700 acres, a bird conservation area and 7.5 miles of marked hiking trails. Hunters may be present October to March 31.

Dwarf Pine Plains,
Sunrise Highway and County Road 31, Westhampton; www.pinebarrens.org.

Long Island is one of only three places in the world with a forest of stunted pitch pines that average 5 to 6 feet tall—none above 8. You may glimpse the rare and beautiful pine barrens bluet damselfly or the white, black, and orange buck moth, which lives solely to procreate and deposits its eggs on the branches of scrub oaks. Access is best in summer. The pine barrens consists of a patchwork of private, county, and state land, so get a map and hiking advice from the Pine Barrens Trail Information Center at (631) 369–9768 (seasonally) or call the Long Island Greenbelt Trail Conference at (631) 360–0753. For information on hiking permits from the New York State Department of Environmental Conservation, call (631) 444–0273.

Edgewood Oak Brush Preserve,
off Commack Road, Deer Park; (631) 444–0273; www.dec.state .ny.us.

Access by New York State Department of Environmental Conservation permit (free). Features 850 acres of pine barrens, 50 acres of open field, a 5-mile trail, and bird-watching (especially hawks).

Gardiner County Park,
Montauk Highway, about a half-mile east of the Robert Moses Causeway, West Bay Shore; (631) 854–0935 (seasonally) or (631) 854–4949; www.co.suffolk.ny.us.

This 231-acre park was once part of the Sagtikos Manor estate. Hikers on any of the 3.5 miles of trails will see beech, black cherry, red maple, pitch pine, and Atlantic white cedars near the road. Approaching the bay are shrub thickets and red cedars. Wetlands include plants such as groundselbush, salt marsh cord grass, and eelgrass.

Garvies Point Museum and Preserve,
50 Barry Drive, Glen Cove; (516) 571–8010; www.co.nassau.ny.us/parkmuse .html.

The wooded cliffs of this sixty-two-acre preserve offer a spectacular view of Hempstead Harbor. Created by a glacial moraine, the area is covered by meadows, thickets, and woodlands with more than fifty species of native and non-native trees such as black cherry, oak, box elder, beech, sassafras, and big tooth aspen. Look for woodchucks, opossums, raccoons, and red foxes in the woods.

Heckscher State Park,
Heckscher Parkway, East Islip; (631) 581–2100; http://nysparks .state.ny.us.

A third of this 1,700-acre park is woodlands, much of it maritime oak and pine. Deer, red foxes, muskrats, and cottontail rabbits

Mushrooms in May at Garvies Point Preserve in Glen Cove

are common; the elusive mink is present. In October the park is a stopover for migrating monarch butterflies.

Hither Hills State Park, off Montauk Highway (Route 27), 4 miles west of Montauk Village; (631) 668–2554; http://nysparks .state.ny.us.

This 1,755-acre park features trails, freshwater pond and Atlantic Ocean beach, the "walking dunes" of Napeague Harbor, and woods with Russian olive, oak, shad, and pine trees. Call ahead for details on the public campground.

Hofstra Arboretum, 1200B Phillips Hall, Hofstra University, Hempstead; (516) 463–6504; www.hofstra.edu.

Take a self-guided tour of one hundred labeled trees spread across Hofstra's 238-acre campus. A sensory garden for disabled visitors features plants at wheelchair level and a water element for sound. The New American Garden on the north campus features perennials and ornamental grasses, which are labeled. A guide map is available. Some trees rarely found on the East Coast include a metasequoia, the bald cypress, the dragon eye, and the tamyosho.

Hoyt Farm Park Preserve, New Highway, Commack; (631) 543–7804.

Features 133 acres with dogwood, oak, and hickory trees. Reproduction of Long Island wigwam, domestic animals; nature center open 1:00 to 4:00 P.M. daily, Memorial Day to Labor Day. Parking free with town resident sticker, $5.00 for nonresidents; parking for disabled at picnic pavilion. Managed by the Town of Smithtown; open year-round.

Islip Greenbelt County Preserve, Nichols Road and Long Island Motor Parkway, Islip; (631) 854–4949.

Preserve features 153 acres and links parts of the Long Island Greenbelt Trail. Access to Lakeland County and Hidden Pond Parks.

Leeds Pond Preserve, 1526 North Plandome Road, Manhasset; (516) 627–9400.

Operated by the Science Museum of Long Island, this thirty-six-acre site includes marked and unmarked trails and sixteen acres of oak, maple, and tulip trees akin to the hardwood forests that once blanketed the northern half of Long Island.

Linda Gronlund Memorial Nature Preserve, Route 114, west of East Hampton Co-op Area, Sag Harbor; (631) 444–0273.

Formerly the Barcelona Neck State Park and Preserve. Wander through more than 340 acres of undisturbed wooded peninsula surrounded by salt marshes. In the upland woods at least half the trees are more than fifty years old. Rare plants include the bushy rockrose, the marsh fimbry, and the beach knotweed. The diamond-back terrapin and the Southern leopard frog live here. Be sure to climb one of the three large hills that offer spectacular overlooks. Access with free seasonal permit available from the New York State Department of Environmental Conservation.

Mashomack Preserve, 79 South Ferry Road, Route 114, Shelter Island; (631) 749–1001; www.nature.org.

This Nature Conservancy preserve offers something for everyone, with more than 2,000 acres of oak woodlands, marshes, freshwater ponds, tidal creeks,

The Red Trail at Mashomack Preserve on Shelter Island

and 10 miles of coastline. Trails range in length from 1.5 to 11 miles. Along the way see white-tailed deer, muskrats, foxes, raccoons, Eastern chipmunks, gray squirrels, and the harmless ribbon snake. Fourteen hundred acres of upland oak and beech trees are developing into an old-growth forest. Other trees include the maple and dogwood. The Pine Swamp Complex is composed of plants rooted in a floating mat of sphagnum moss, 10 feet thick in places, and dating back four millennia. The swamp is a good place to see water willow, swamp azalea, high-bush blueberry, white alder, and winterberry and mountain holly.

Look for a stand of white pines that shelters two state-protected orchids—the whorled pogonia and the pink lady's slipper.

Massapequa Preserve, between Merrick Road and Linden Street, Massapequa Park; (516) 571-7443.

Visit 423 acres of undeveloped woodlands, ponds, lakes, and wetlands bordering Massapequa Creek. The property once belonged to the New York City water supply, but was purchased by Nassau County in 1981. The preserve is home to the largest pine barrens tract in Nassau County and includes 5 miles of the Long Island Greenbelt Trail.

Mill Pond County Park, Merrick Road and Abby Court, Bellmore Village; (516) 572-0290.

Stroll around the lake and then venture into the mature woodlands, which offer large white and black oaks, sweet gums, black cherries and flowering dogwoods. Highbush blueberries blossom in summer.

Muttontown Preserve, Muttontown Lane, East Norwich; (516) 571-8500; www.co.nassau .ny.us/parkmuse.html.

At 550 acres, this is one of Nassau County's largest natural areas. It has 10 miles of nature trails and 20 miles of bridle paths. Look for Japanese red maple; red spruce; scots pine; white, red, and black oak; black and gray birch; and flowering dogwood. Edible American persimmons grow on trees at Persimmon Pond. Other edible plants include sheep and wood sorrel, wild carrots, and crab apples. The endangered tiger salamander—one of the largest terrestrial salamanders in the country at 7 to 8 inches long—has been reintroduced into the preserve's ponds.

Nissequogue River State Park,

St. Johnland Road, Kings Park; (631) 269–4927; http://nysparks .state.ny.us.

The park encompasses 153 acres along the Nissequogue River. Woodlands include old oak, Norway and sycamore maple, bitternut and mockernut hickory, black walnut, catalpa, and gray birch.

Oceanside Marine Nature Study Area, 500 Slice Drive, Oceanside; (516) 766–1580; www.townofhempstead.org.

This fifty-two-acre sanctuary opened on the very first Earth Day in 1970. Cross the boardwalks over the wetlands to spot beach plum, silverberry, black locust, and even edible sumac. Along the drier trails scarlet oaks, cherries, and pitch pines grow.

Orr Preserve, 130 Bayview Avenue, East Islip; (631) 224–5436.

Managed by the South Shore Nature Center, the preserve offers trails, a boardwalk, a

stream, and a freshwater pond. Red maple and black tupelo trees line the stream and boardwalk; black cherry and white and black oak occupy the drier northeastern sections. You might spot deer and smaller mammals, as well as reptiles and amphibians.

Planting Fields Arboretum State Historic Park, Planting Fields Road, Oyster Bay; (516) 922–8600; www.plantingfields.org.

Once the estate of insurance magnate William Robertson Coe, the arboretum's 400 acres include gardens, woodland paths, and impressive plant collections. While here, see the majestic copper beech tree that Coe presented to his wife Mai in 1915. (See "Our Favorites" in this chapter.) Other transplants to these grounds include Italian wall lizards descended from those believed to have escaped from a broken crate bound for a Garden City pet store in 1967. Look for the lizards from October through March.

Poxabogue County Park, Old Farm Road north of Montauk Highway, Bridgehampton; (631) 854–4949; www.suffolk countyny.gov.

Features twenty-six acres, a half-mile nature walk, and waterfowl.

Prosser Pines County Preserve, Yaphank–Middle Island Road, south of Route 25, Middle Island; (631) 852–5500; www.co.suffolk.ny.us.

A grove of lesser celandine at the Muttontown Preserve in East Norwich

Don't be confused by the name of the adjacent Cathedral Pines County Park, a haven for cyclists and campers. At Prosser Pines you'll find a small forest, or cathedral, of towering white pines, remnants of a nineteenth-century plantation. Take the trail at the far end of the parking lot and you'll soon find a canopy of mammoth evergreens, a soft bed of pine needles cushioning your steps.

Quogue Wildlife Refuge, County Road 104 to Old Country Road, Quogue; (631) 653–4771; www .quoguerefuge.com.

A snapping turtle at Quogue Wildlife Refuge, a 300-acre preserve on the East End

The refuge is one of several spots where you can reach Long Island's dwarf pine plains. Five miles of trails along 300 acres take you into the woods, where you'll see pitch pine and scarlet, white, black, and bear oaks. Look for American holly, inkberry, winterberry, blueberry, huckleberry, and bayberry. The refuge is home to more than seventy species of wildflowers and carnivorous plants such as the pitcher plant and sundew.

Rocky Point Natural Resources Management Area, north on Route 216 to Whiskey Road, Rocky Point; (631) 444–0273; www.dec.state.ny.us.

Planning is needed to hike this 5,000-acre pine barrens forest. Call the Long Island Greenbelt Trail Conference for a free state hiking permit and trail advice at (631) 360–0753. With 10.3 miles of marked trails, this preserve opens the door to a rare ecosystem of dwarfed trees. Here you'll find pitch pine, bear oak, blueberry, huckleberry, and sheep laurel.

Sands Point Preserve, 95 Middle Neck Road, Sands Point; (516) 571–7900; www.sandspointpreserve.org.

The opulent Gold Coast architecture of the preserve's Falaise Mansion and Castlegould is no match for the beauty of its 216 acres of forests, meadows, lawns, shore cliffs, and freshwater pond. Six self-guided nature trails total 5 miles. See red maple, birch, American holly, white and black oak, and sassafras trees. Descendants of black locust trees planted in the 1700s by settler John Sands survive near the pond. In the forest mature oaks reach 80 feet and some are almost 200 years old. Viburnums and spicebush are common forest shrubs. Raccoons, rabbits, squirrels, moles, and shrews inhabit the forests and meadows. Look for horseshoe crabs, calico crabs, spider crabs, moon snails, razor clams, and whelk egg cases at the shore.

Sears Bellows County Park, Bellows Pond Road, Flanders; (631) 852–8290; www.suffolkcountyny.gov.

The park's 693 acres feature camping by reservation, rowboat rentals, bridle paths with rentals, protected beach, freshwater fishing, waterfowl, and deer.

Shadmoor State Park, Route 27 and Seaside Avenue, Montauk; (631) 668–3781; http://nysparks.state.ny.us.

This ninety-nine-acre park offers ocean beach, freshwater wetlands, and hiking and biking trails. Black cherry trees and the rare sandplain gerardia plant grow here.

South Shore Nature Center, 130 Bayview Avenue, East Islip; (631) 224–5436; http://estuary.cog.ny.us/access_guide/site49.html.

March snow at Sands Point

Native to Asia, sika deer in the Carmans River in Southaven County Park in Yaphank

The center features 206 acres of upland and wetland woods, a freshwater pond, salt marsh, and a 2.3-mile hiking trail. In the upland woods are black gum, sassafras, red maple, black cherry, and white and black oaks. In the wetland woods and thickets, American holly, sweet pepperbush, swamp honeysuckle, and swamp azalea grow. At the freshwater pond look for frogs, painted and snapping turtles, and muskrats. Deer and red foxes sometimes frequent the marsh.

Southaven County Park, William Floyd Parkway, west on to Victory Avenue, Yaphank; (631) 854–1414; www.co.suffolk.ny.us.

View 3 miles of the scenic Carmans River on foot or horseback. Equestrians and hikers enjoy 7 miles of marked and unmarked trails on 1,356 acres. In the woods closest to the park's facilities, red, black, white, and bear oak grow. To the north a pine barrens forest emerges. Near the river red maple, see pepperbush and skunk cabbage. The park is home to opossums, raccoons, chipmunks, and squirrels.

Sunken Forest, Sailors Haven, across Great South Bay from Sayville, on the Fire Island National Seashore; (631) 597–6183; www.nps.gov/fiis.

The Sunken Forest is one of the last remaining maritime forests on the East Coast, with trees older than 200 years. Since the trees developed behind a line of secondary dunes, they appear sunken below the dunes. Trees average 20 to 30 feet tall and only a foot wide, many impossibly gnarled and twisted. The forest, about forty acres, consists primarily of American holly, sassafras, and shadblow. On the 1.5-mile boardwalk trail, you may spot white-tailed deer, red foxes, meadow voles, and box turtles.

Tackapausha County Preserve, Washington Avenue, Seaford; (516) 571–7443; www.co.nassau.ny.us/parkmuse.html.

In the midst of suburbia lies a strip of woodlands only 1,000 feet wide and 1.5 miles long surrounding Seaford Creek. Despite the size, the preserve has plenty to offer. The largest stand of the rare Atlantic white cedar in the United States grows here. Also see red maple and white oak, swamp azalea, spicebush, sweet pepperbush, and scarlet oak. A museum has trail maps and historical information.

Terrell River County Park, off Montauk Highway, Center Moriches; (631) 854–4949.

Formerly the Havens Estate, this 263-acre preserve was purchased by Suffolk County in 1986 to avoid development and protect Moriches Bay. Managed by the Moriches Bay Audubon Society, the preserve's young forest holds white oak, Atlantic white cedar, and prickly ash. A more mature forest of scarlet, white, and black oaks; sassafras; and catbrier gives way to find pitch pine, American holly, Atlantic white cedar, and gray birch closer to the bay. Near the beach a wall of cedars opens up to a freshwater marsh, salt marsh, and the bay.

Tiffany Creek Preserve, Sandy Hill Road, Oyster Bay; (516) 571–8500; www.co.nassau .ny.us/parkmuse.html.

This forty-five-acre preserve is accessible to the public in the parcel west of Sandy Hill Road. A self-guided nature trail leads through a forest with black, red, and scarlet oaks.

Trail View State Park, Jericho Turnpike, one-quarter-mile west of Woodbury Road, Woodbury; (631) 423–1770.

This linear park has trails for hiking, cycling, and birding throughout its 400 acres. A 7.4-mile stretch of the Nassau–Suffolk Trail passes through.

Twin Lakes Preserve, Old Mill Road and Park Avenue, Wantagh; (516) 766–1580; www.townof hempstead.org.

Animal tracks on a snowy January day at Welwyn Preserve in Glen Cove

This Town of Hempstead preserve offers four ponds, 1.8 miles of trails, and a charming footbridge overlooking Bellmore Creek. In the woods and near the ponds, you'll see sassafras, red and Norway maples, dogwood, sweet gum, black cherry, black oak, and tupelo. Plants that attract wildlife include blackberry, blueberry, catbrier, grape, and wild rose.

Welwyn Preserve, Crescent Beach Road, Glen Cove; (516) 571–8500.

Four marked trails lead you through more than 200 acres of wooded stream valley, freshwater ponds and swamps, and salt marsh. The swamp forest is home to one of the finest stands of old-growth tulip trees on Long Island, some higher than 100 feet.

Wertheim National Wildlife Refuge, 300 Smith Road, off Montauk Highway, Shirley; (631) 286–0485; http://wertheim .fws.gov.

The lower Carmans River runs through this 2,600-acre refuge. Deer and red foxes are sometimes seen on the water's edge. Be on the lookout for minks, weasels, and muskrats, along with flying squirrels and bats using staff-made nest boxes. One nature trail begins at the refuge headquarters, and another is accessible only by boat (downstream from headquarters on the right, marked by an INDIAN LANDING TRAIL sign). A good portion of the refuge is oak and pine-oak woodlands. Common trees include scarlet, black, red, and white oaks; pitch pine; and black cherry. Autumn visitors enjoy spectacular scarlet foliage of red maple and black gum in the wooded swamps.

West Hills County Park, Sweet Hollow Road, Huntington; (631) 854–4423; www.suffolkcountyny.gov.

On 854 acres are groomed nature trails, including the his-toric Walt Whitman Trail to Jayne's Hill, Long Island's highest point, about 400 feet. Trails boast wild mountain laurel, moccasin flower, fern species, salamanders, turtles, chipmunks, squirrels, and red foxes.

Westhampton Management Area, Route 31 near Suffolk County Airport, Westhampton; (631) 444–0273.

Access by free New York State Department of Environmental Conservation permit. Features 277 acres of dwarf pitch pine and scrub oak.

Long Island's Best-known Trails

A wealth of information on Long Island hiking is available at www.hike-li.com.

Long Island Greenbelt Trail, 32 miles along the Connetquot and Nissequogue Rivers.

This winding trail goes from Heckscher State Park on the Great South Bay to Sunken Meadow bluffs on the Sound. White-tailed deer, wild turkeys, and native plants can be seen. Access points include Connetquot River State Park Preserve on the south (Sunrise and Montauk Highways); on the north Caleb Smith State Park Preserve, Jericho Turnpike between the Smithtown bull statue and Old Willets Path (preserve closed Monday and Tuesday); and Nissequogue River State Park on St. Johnland Road. Other access:

Heckscher State Park (field 8), Sunken Meadow State Park (field 3), and Blydenburgh County Park (New Mill Road) on the north.

Long Island Pine Barrens Trail, encompassing nearly 50 miles of foot paths in eastern Suffolk.

Meanders past maple swamps, ponds, and overlooks, extending from Rocky Point to Shinnecock Canal through the pine barrens. Includes Rocky Point Preserve, Pine Trail Preserve, Peconic River watershed, Maple Swamp, and Sears Bellows County Park. A written permit is required to hike parts of the trail or to park a vehicle; call the New York State Department of Environmental Conservation at (631) 444–0273. Other access: Pine Trail Preserve parking area on Route 25, half-mile east of William Floyd Parkway. The trail is part of the 130-mile Paumanok Path from Rocky Point to Shinnecock Canal; it has a few links in Southampton and leads from East Hampton border to Montauk Point. Write to Greenbelt Trail Conference, P.O. Box 5636, Hauppauge 11788. Or stop at the Pine Barrens Trail Information Center, Long Island Expressway, exit 70, Manorville.

Nassau–Suffolk Trail, 20 miles between Massapequa Preserve on the South Shore and Cold Spring Harbor on the north.

See hawks, foxes, and mountain laurel. Main entrance is at Ocean Avenue, north of Merrick Road, in Massapequa. Trail follows Carroon's Lake shore through soap

An entrance to the Walt Whitman Trail in Huntington

Walt Whitman Trail, 8 miles from the Whitman birthplace through West Hills County Park, Sweet Hollow Road, Huntington; (631) 854–4423.

Circular trail includes Jayne's Hill, the highest point on Long Island. Trail links up with the Nassau–Suffolk Trail.

Hiking Clubs

Adirondack Mountain Club, 5 Tudor Drive, Stony Brook; (516) 354–0231, before 9:00 P.M.; www.adkli.org.

Meets 8:00 P.M. the second Thursday of the month September to June (except October) at St. Elizabeth's Parish Hall, 175 Wolf Hill Road, Melville. Offers educational programs; easy-to-strenuous weekly outings; and backpacking with seasonal options on Long Island, the Hudson Valley, Catskills, and Adirondacks. Carpooling available.

East Hampton Trails Preservation Society, P.O. Box 2144, Amagansett 11930; (631) 329–4227; www.hike-li.com.

Free hikes Wednesday and Saturday year-round.

Group for the South Fork, P.O. Box 569, Bridgehampton 11932; (631) 537–1400; www.thehamptons.com/group.

More than forty hikes a year.

bush and swamp maples to a log bridge, where vegetation begins to change to pine barrens. Later, the trail cuts near the Bethpage Parkway. The Cold Spring Harbor end is at Route 25A; a parking area is on the south side.

Northwest Path, a 6-mile path in East Hampton; part of the Paumanok Path; (631) 324–4143.

Start at Route 114 at Edwards Hole Road. Yellow triangles to Bull Path mark the blazed portion. The trail has areas of oak and hickory forest and blueberry and huckleberry bushes among pitch pine and mountain laurel. West of Bull Path are white pine groves. At trail's end are wetlands with abundant foliage, deer, and red-tailed hawks. Closed November to March; call for accessibility other times. The town clerk sells maps. Call the number above or visit the clerk's office at

159 Pantiago Road in East Hampton, 9:00 A.M. to 4:00 P.M. weekdays or 9:00 A.M. to noon the first Saturday of each month.

Red Creek Park, a 5-mile loop in Red Creek Town Park, Southampton; (631) 728–8585.

Spotted and red-tailed hawks, blue heron, pheasant, deer, kettle holes, pitch pine, maple, tupelo, and, in October, monarch butterflies can be seen. Maps are available at park entrance on Old Riverhead Road, off Route 24, in Hampton Bays.

Stump Pond Trail, a 5-mile trail begins at the Long Island Greenbelt Trail office at Blydenburgh County Park, Smithtown; (631) 360–0753; www.hike-li.com/ligtc.

The trail winds around the 164-acre Stump Pond. Tours of historic area offered Saturdays at 1:00 P.M. Call to confirm.

Members of the Long Island Greenbelt Trail Conference at Blydenburgh County Park in Smithtown

ing, and outdoor activities on and off Long Island.

Seatuck Environmental Association, P.O. Box 31, Islip 11751; (631) 581–6908; www.seatuck .org.

Hikes, preschool and singles programs, monthly lectures.

Southampton Trails Preservation Society, P.O. Box 1171, Bridgehampton 11932; (631) 537–5202; www.hike-li.com.

Hikes every Saturday and Sunday year-round and two Thursdays a month in summer.

In Captivity

Town of Brookhaven Ecology Site, Park and Animal Preserve, 249 Buckley Road, Holtsville; (631) 758–9664.

The site includes a greenhouse, exercise trails, park, and petting zoo. The animal preserve houses more than one hundred injured or nonreleasable wild animals and farm animals for viewing and educational programs. Tours available.

Volunteers for Wildlife Hospital and Education Center, Caumsett State Historic Park, 25 Lloyd Harbor Road, Lloyd Neck; (631) 423–0982; www.volunteers forwildlife.org.

Injured animals are rehabilitated here or kept for public education programs.

Long Island Greenbelt Trail Conference, P.O. Box 5636, Hauppauge 11788; (631) 360–0753; www.hike-li.com.

The nonprofit group develops and maintains trails. Membership fee. Pathfinder membership includes maps. Conducts more than 150 guided hikes a year and Saturday tours at 1:00 P.M. at the Blydenburgh–Weld House, Blydenburgh County Park north entrance, New Mill Road, Smithtown.

Long Island Orienteering Club, (631) 567–5063; www.geography .hunter.cuny.edu/~tbw/lioc.

Meetings rotate among Sunken Meadow and Caumsett State Parks, West Hills County Park, and Muttontown Preserve. Noncompetitive. Membership fee. Waiver forms required if younger than eighteen.

Nassau Hiking and Outdoor Club, P.O. Box 321, Lawrence 11559; (631) 842–4733; www.nhoc.org.

Meets at 8:00 P.M. the third Tuesday of the month (except August and January) at the special events center, Eisenhower Park, East Meadow. Offers conservation activities, hiking, bik-

A shark with a broken fishing line in its mouth swimming 28 miles off Montauk Point

The Sea, Sound, and Shore

By Joe Haberstroh

Long Island is a place of pocket wildernesses with one, sparkling exception—the sea and the shore.

The marine environment moderates the climate here and even salts the air, especially along the South Shore. The sea and the shore offer Long Island's last untrammeled tracts, and beneath the sea, a parade of wildlife—great whales and microscopic shrimp and migrating eels.

The water does not simply provide the blue frames for picture postcards of Long Island. The sea and shore are dynamic, and discoveries are to be made throughout the year. Around Thanksgiving every year Caribbean-born sea turtles that have spent the autumn in local waters routinely wait too long to return south and wash up on beaches, stunned from the cold. A mid-January day might find one hundred healthy seals hauled up on sand shoals in Hempstead, Moriches, and Shinnecock Bays. In midsummer more than twenty-five species of sharks will have migrated to Long Island waters, along with whales,

A leatherback turtle fitted with a transmitter in Puerto Rico before spring migration; sea turtles swim north to Long Island from the Caribbean

which feed here before pushing north to the colder water they prefer.

Long Island's more than 1,180 miles of shoreline hug small embayments in the Peconic Estuary, Long Island Sound, and, of course, the Atlantic Ocean. Regeneration is a theme here: Lobsters cut up in a fight on the bottom of the Sound simply regrow their limbs; fish eat snails and crustaceans on the bottom of the ocean and the dead animals' shells are rolled ashore by the tides and made part of the dunes; and the shore itself is under continual remodeling, as 10,000 waves rinse and reshape the beach each day.

Even in the wash of the surf, life abounds. On the rocks at Montauk, sea lettuce, Irish moss, and several kinds of seaweed cling to the hard surfaces. A nuisance to surfers and those who stroll the shoreline, the seaweed provides food and protective cover for fish, crabs, clams, and shrimp.

It can all seem a bit otherworldly, the way crabs pry open clams and hermit crabs carry the shells of dead animals on their backs instead of building their own. But these are the natural ways of the sea and the shore.

Access can be had for the price of a ticket on a whale watch cruise, Great South Bay ferry, or charter fishing boat. Long Island's shores are also threaded with numerous hiking trails that shadow the water-washed undulations along the shore. The contrasts can be sublime. Within an hour's drive you can enjoy quiet Peconic Bay views from the pebbly trails of Elizabeth A. Morton

A hermit crab from Cold Spring Harbor in the shell of another creature

National Wildlife Refuge, near Sag Harbor, and march beside the crashing Atlantic surf at "Road K," one of the hottest local surfing beaches, just west of Shinnecock Inlet.

It's difficult to imagine when Long Island was untamed. Under our roads are horse trails and under the trails are paths worn in the woods by Native American hunting parties. But the sea and shore comprise the Island's last true wilderness, its great blue beyond.

(Left) Clam shells at Jones Beach; (Above) A lone sailboat on Long Island Sound, near Eaton's Neck

Horseshoe Crabs

What: Among the ancients of Long Island's fauna, these crabs move ashore every spring to mate. Over the course of the season, the females arrive onshore several times with high tides. With five sets of legs, horseshoe crabs are more closely related to spiders or scorpions than other crabs.

When: Mating takes place in late May, early June.

Where: Among many sites, the muddy shoreline adjacent to the Jones Beach State Park boat basin, on the park's west end.

Keep in Mind: Give them space. Horseshoe crabs, whose population has been in decline because they are used for bait, are a cause for concern. Their eggs provide food for migrating shorebirds, some of which are endangered.

Horseshoe crabs—living fossils, some say—at Jones Beach

Seals

What: Migrating from as far north as the Arctic, four species of seals make winter homes around Long Island. They are harp, harbor, hooded, and gray seals, with harbor seals the most common.

When: Low tide is the best time to see the seals climb out of the water to rest on rocky outcroppings or sandbars.

Where: Montauk Point, at the wooden blind on the bluff about a half-mile west of the point, on the north shore. At Cupsogue County Park (adjacent to West Hampton Dunes), use the dirt road that heads west toward Moriches Inlet, and take up positions along the bay shore, on the north side of the road.

Keep in Mind: Seals are people-shy. To view them up close, it's best to keep quiet, keep low, and limit sudden movements.

Harbor seals on the rocks of Block Island Sound, near Montauk

The Sunken Forest

What: Rare, 300-year-old maritime forest on Fire Island dominated by American holly. There is a storybook flavor here: The salt spray blasting from the nearby ocean stunts the trees' growth, creating a ceiling effect where most of the trees are the same height. A wooden boardwalk runs through the forest.

When: Anytime, but in winter many of the trees in the forty-acre woods lose their leaves, and the ferryboats reduce service from the South Shore across the Great South Bay to the Fire Island National Seashore.

Where: For ferry schedules to Fire Island, call (631) 589–8980. The Sailors Haven visitor center, operated by the National Park Service, is open May through October.

Keep in Mind: Besides the holly the other common tree in the Sunken Forest is sassafras. Its leaves are strange: On a single tree, some leaves might be shaped like mittens, others have three prongs, and still others are unfaceted and oval-shaped.

The boardwalk through the Sunken Forest on Fire Island

Walking Dunes

What: These unusual landforms, overlooking Napeague Harbor between Amagansett and Montauk, change their shape and location with the winds. The 80-foot dunes ripple across a valley that covers an area about 1 mile wide and 4 miles long. Depending on wind strength, the withered trunks of an old woods—pitch pine and black oak—could be uncovered. Wild orchids are here and a few cranberries, too.

When: Year-round.

Where: Best access is through Hither Hills State Park; call (631) 668–2554. The dunes are along the eastern boundary of the park.

Keep in Mind: Scenes from Rudolph Valentino's 1921 film *The Sheik* were filmed at the dunes.

The walking dunes at Hither Hills State Park on the east side of Napeague Harbor, north on Montauk Highway; the dunes migrate with the winds, sometimes revealing long-buried trees

A humpback whale in the Atlantic, 24 miles off Montauk

Whales

What: Long Island lies in the migratory path of several species of whales. Common types here are humpback, Northern right, minke, sei, and finback. Occasionally, whales can be sighted from South Shore beaches. Whales in the Island's waters measure 30 to 60 feet long and weigh thirty to forty tons. A few times a year, a sick whale strands itself on a local beach.

When: Usually in the summer months.

Where: Along the South Shore and, most predictably, off Montauk. The Coastal Research and Education Society of Long Island offers New York State's only whale-watching cruises. Call (631) 244–3352.

Keep in Mind: The society has day trips and fifty-one-hour trips, with meals and accommodations provided. On the two-day trips, the boat commonly travels more than 100 miles offshore.

Seashells
Treasures from the Tides

The discarded homes of scallops, clams, and other mollusks wash up by the millions on Long Island's beaches. Currents sometimes bring New England's ocean residents to the rocky beaches of Montauk, while tropical species sometimes travel along the Gulf Stream from the south.

You can beachcomb year-round, as certain seashells seem to predominate at different times. For example, enthusiasts can see Northern moon snails at Montauk's Ditch Plains in May, scallops at Greenport around Columbus Day, and Atlantic plate limpits along Orient Beach State Park in December. And in late summer or early fall at Jones Beach, you might see the coquina, a colorful bivalve that is brought up with the Gulf Stream but unable to survive the harsher winters here.

A Field Guide to Long Island's Seashore is a good resource for beginners and is available through the Museum of Long Island Natural Sciences at Stony Brook University; call (631) 632–8230. For enthusiasts the Long Island Shell Club hosts occasional meetings and outings. For details call Mel Springer at (516) 785–8211.

A word to the wise: Limiting your collection to unoccupied shells is not only more environmentally friendly but also much easier on your nose.

**Slipper shells found on
Long Island beaches**

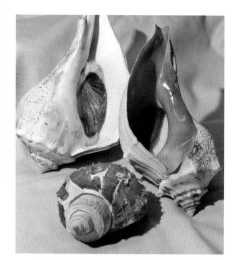

Channeled Whelk

Channeled whelk, 3½ to 7½ inches long, is flanked by two knobbed whelk, 4 to 9 inches long. The left shell is a "rare" left-handed whelk.

Brown-banded Wentletraps

Brown-banded wentletraps, ⅜ to 1 inch long, are very rare. In the 1960s, New York State halted plans to dredge the Great South Bay near Islip when they were found there.

Variable Coquina

Variable coquina, sometimes used in chowder, can be found at Jones Beach and are ⅓ to 1 inch long.

Bay Scallops

Bay scallops, 1½ to 4 inches long, are fished commercially and found in Peconic Bay.

Surf Clams

Surf clams, 1¾ to 9 inches long, are common along the South Shore.

Eastern Oyster

Eastern oyster, 2 to 8 inches long, is a delicacy. Shells are usually found near bays.

False Angel Wings

False angel wings, which are found on coastal beaches, are 1 to 2 inches long.

Fossilized Northern Moon Snail

Fossilized northern moon snail, found at Jones Beach, is about 2 inches high.

Atlantic Oyster Drills

Atlantic oyster drills, ½ to 1¾ inches long, are predators and are found in bays, Long Island Sound, and the Atlantic Ocean.

The Truth about Sharks

John Morrissey, an associate professor of biology at Hofstra University, has studied sharks around the world. As a boy he planned to be a paleontologist. Then in 1975 he saw the movie *Jaws*.

Q. How many different kinds of sharks are in the ocean around Long Island?

A. About forty to fifty that live in shallow enough water for us to bump into.

Q. How are they doing?

A. They're in very bad shape. There is a woman, Julia Baum, who is up in Nova Scotia, and she and her colleagues published a paper in which she estimated that sharks in the western Atlantic have declined on average by 61 percent in just fifteen years, from 1986 to 2000. Among the biggies, white sharks have dropped 79 percent, threshers have dropped 79 percent, hammerheads have dropped 89 percent. I did my masters here in the early 1980s, and the local tournaments were very generous to those of us who wanted to come down and look at what those in the tournaments had caught. Bay Shore has 250 boats, four anglers per boat . . . so the effort is the same year after year. When I was there in the eighties, the fishermen were bringing in about 200 blue sharks per day. I got hired here in 1991, and so I went back to Bay Shore in the summer of 1992. They landed 26 blue sharks.

In his office at Hofstra University, biologist John Morrissey with a shark's jaw

Q. Beyond the intrinsic value that many people place on sharks, what's the ecological significance of the possibility that we are losing our sharks?

A. I don't know, and, in my opinion, anyone who will tell you they know is foolish. But I can assure you, things will be different. When you remove all the predators, the balance of power changes. For all I know the result could be beneficial. In South Africa, in the 1950s, they had a problem with shark attacks, so they set up a system of gill nets offshore. Attacks decreased greatly because they were destroying this population of large sharks, which were the ones attacking people. What happened was, their fisheries collapsed. The reason was, the small coastal sharks skyrocketed, and they in turn focused on their normal prey, which are the things we like to eat.

Q. Are sharks intelligent?

A. They are. Relative to rats and rabbits, they learn much, much faster. [In experiments in which animals are trained to memorize a maze] it takes rats and rabbits many more trials to get it. Also, sharks retain it. If in about four months you put the rat or rabbit in the maze that it previously ran expertly, it will look at you confused, like, "What do you want me to do?" Sharks remember for eight or nine months after being removed from the maze.

Q. What are the myths about sharks that drive you crazy?

A. Certainly that they are dumb. And it's a myth that attacks are motivated by hunger. A shark attack is completely analogous to you getting bitten by my dog on my lawn. Tissue is not removed. They bite once and swim away.

Basking sharks on a June day in the Atlantic, about a mile off Georgica Beach in East Hampton

Q. Tissue is not removed? People get their arms chewed off. What do you mean?

A. Ninety-two percent of the time, tissue is not removed. If sharks were truly feeding on us, the oceans would be red.

Q. You are routinely in the water where sharks are present, yes?

A. I've been in the water with twenty to thirty reef sharks at a time.

Q. Doesn't that make you uncomfortable?

A. No. I guess because I trust my opinion that they don't eat us. We've only been in the water for one hundred years. It's unlikely that they have learned we are food.

Q. How long have they been in the water?

A. Between forty and eighty million years.

Q. What did you think about the movie *Jaws*?

A. It's responsible for my career. I was a paleontology buff until I saw that movie. It literally changed my life. I just thought the shark was the underdog in that movie, and I have always rooted for the underdog. I thought, sharks need an advocate.

Q. And, were you disappointed that your introduction to sharks, in the movie, turned out to be baseless in fact?

A. No. I clearly have this affection for primitive animals. And sharks are primitive animals. They predate dinosaurs.

Q. Do you have a favorite shark?

A. Yeah, oh yeah. Nurse sharks are my favorite in terms of their personality, if I can use that word. They're so cute and friendly. I had one in captivity once. A little baby, a foot and a half long, in water 10 inches deep, in a lab. It would ask me for food the same way your cat or dog does, and only me. If I was tardy in terms of feeding it, it would come over to the side of the tank, it would clamber up on its pectoral fins, and it would spit a stream of water right at me. Hit me right in the side, as I walked by. No one else got spit at. It knew me.

—JOE HABERSTROH

Four Steps in the Development of a Lobster

(Left) A female lobster carries fertilized eggs under her tail. Of 10,000 eggs that she may release, perhaps only 10 will survive. After release the larvae swim freely for several weeks. Mosquito-size, they bob up and down near the water's surface; they are called "bugs."

(Bottom, left) Appendages begin to show on two very young lobsters. The larger one is about as long as a grain of rice. In its first two to four weeks, a lobster will shed its shell three times.

(Bottom, right) Calipers are used to measure a juvenile lobster off Northport. In its first year a young lobster will eat organisms that pass through its seafloor shelter. With growth, lobsters venture out to find food.

(Right) Mark Phillips of Alice's Fish Market in Greenport shows off a mature lobster. A lobster's smaller claw is used for cutting, the larger for crushing. Lobsters can live for fifty years.

Life of a Squid

What sees the unseen, shifts its appearance at will, has a secret escape weapon, and can hurtle across the ocean at 30 mph?

Meet the squid, the closest thing to a comic book superhero in Long Island's waters.

The most common local variety is the longfin squid, or *Loligo pealeii*, a ten-tentacled cephalopod found in bays, such as the Peconic, and in coastal waters. Measuring 12 to 16 inches long, these squid are a staple of the fishing industry and a scientific wonder.

"Your lovely little calamari that you use for bait has a big and complicated brain," said Roger Hanlon, a senior scientist at the Marine Biological Laboratory in Woods Hole, Massachusetts. The brain is big because it presides over a complex range of behaviors.

Social animals that live in schools, squid communicate by flashing different patterns on their skin. A female signals her sexual availability to males by making rings around her body and dropping her tentacles; hot-to-trot males display aggression toward other suitors by shooting a flame-like pattern up their sides. They also camouflage themselves from predators by mimicking their backgrounds.

Squid taken from Peconic Bay

Large nerve cells help squid relay these pattern changes quickly, said Keith Serafy, a professor of biology and marine sciences at Southampton College. They also help with jet propulsion, a technique that squid use to elude predators or chase prey. They siphon in water, sealing it off in a cavity with a muscular flap, then expel it through a sort of nozzle, which pushes them rapidly through the water.

When a squid is backed into a corner, it shoots a dark, nontoxic ink at its pursuer and darts away. Bluefish, weakfish, striped bass, and even a few types of whales appear to enjoy calamari as much as we do. But squid are busy predators in their own right, trolling the water for prey with their twin, long, feeding tentacles outstretched. Unlucky fish are nabbed, then rendered immobile with a bite from the squid's parrotlike beak.

Squid have the ability to see polarized light, which allows them to easily spot prey species, such as larval fish or small crustaceans, which look transparent to us—as well as to most other aquatic predators. It's just one more evolutionary edge that keeps squid competitive in what Hanlon characterizes as an ever-changing "arms race" between predator and prey.

—JENNIFER SMITH

AT THE BEACH

By Laura Mann

Access to many municipal beaches is restricted. Call ahead for details on beach access, fees, parking, pets, and rules for fishing and water sports. Many other Long Island beaches appear in "On the Rivers and Bays" in Chapter 4.

Atlantic Ocean Beaches

Atlantic Avenue Beach, end of Atlantic Avenue, off Route 27, Amagansett; (631) 324–2417.

Town of East Hampton beach with 700 feet on the Atlantic Ocean.

Camp Hero State Park, Montauk Point State Parkway (Route 27) east to the end, Montauk; (631) 668–5000; http://nys parks.state.ny.us.

Features 415 acres of woods, Atlantic Ocean beachfront, maritime forests, freshwater wetlands, ocean vistas, dramatic bluffs, and an abundance of birds; trails for hiking, biking, and horseback riding; surf fishing with a permit; picnic areas and a former military site.

Cedar Beach, Ocean Parkway, off Wantagh or Robert Moses Parkways, Babylon; (631) 893–2100; www.townofbabylon.com/guides .cfm.

Town of Babylon beach with three-quarters of a mile on the Atlantic Ocean.

An August day on Flying Point Beach in Water Mill

Cupsogue Beach County Park, west end of Dune Road across the inlet from Smith Point County Park, Westhampton; (631) 852–8111, (631) 854–4949 (off-season); www.suffolk countyny.gov.

Suffolk County beach with 1 mile on Moriches Inlet.

Davis Park, opposite Patchogue, Fire Island; (631) 451–6100; www.brookhaven.org.

Town of Brookhaven beach with 800 feet on the Atlantic Ocean.

Ditch Plains, off Ditch Plains Road, Montauk; (631) 324–2417.

Town of East Hampton beach with 500 feet on the Atlantic Ocean.

East Lake Drive Beach, off Route 27 at end of East Lake Drive, Montauk; (631) 324–2417.

Town of East Hampton beach with 300 feet on Block Island Sound.

Eugene Nickerson Beach, Loop Parkway to Lido Boulevard, Lido Beach; (516) 571–7700; www.co.nassau.ny.us.

Nassau County beach with half-mile on the Atlantic Ocean.

Flying Point Beach, Flying Point Road, Water Mill; (631) 728–8585.

Town of Southampton beach with 250 feet on the Atlantic Ocean.

Sanderlings and a lone gull in the surf at Babylon's Gilgo Beach

Georgica Beach, end of Apaquogue Road and Lily Pond Lane, East Hampton; (631) 324–4150.

Village of East Hampton beach with 300 feet on the Atlantic Ocean.

Gilgo Beach, Ocean Parkway, off Wantagh and Robert Moses Parkways, Babylon; (631) 893–2100; www.townofbabylon .com/guides.cfm.

Town of Babylon beach with 7 miles on the Atlantic Ocean.

Great Gun, opposite Center Moriches, Fire Island; (631) 451–6100; www.brookhaven.org.

Town of Brookhaven beach with 800 feet on the Atlantic Ocean.

Hither Hills State Park, off Montauk Highway (Route 27), 4 miles west of Montauk; (631) 668–2554; http://nys parks.state.ny.us.

Nature trails, freshwater pond, and 2.5-mile ocean beach.

Camping along the Atlantic; reservations are necessary. Call (800) 456–CAMP.

Indian Wells Beach, end of Indian Wells Highway, Amagansett; (631) 324–2417.

Town of East Hampton beach with 700 feet on the Atlantic Ocean.

Jones Beach State Park, Ocean Parkway, off south end of Wantagh and Meadowbrook Parkways, Wantagh; (516) 785–1600; http://nysparks.state.ny.us.

Eight ocean beaches and Zachs Bay beach; 2-mile boardwalk; surf chairs for the disabled at fields 2, 6, and Central Mall; beach ramp at field 6; boat basin; surf casting. Theodore Roosevelt Nature Center at the West End 1 area has outdoor/indoor displays, hands-on children's activities, and programs.

Kirk Park Beach, off Route 27, just west of Montauk village; (631) 324–2417.

Town of East Hampton beach with 500 feet on the Atlantic Ocean.

Lido Beach, 630 Lido Boulevard, Lido Beach; (516) 431–6650; www.townofhempstead.org.

Town of Hempstead beach with 1,554 feet on the Atlantic Ocean.

Main Beach, end of Ocean Avenue, off Montauk Highway, East Hampton; (631) 324–0074, in summer.

Village of East Hampton beach with 300 feet on the Atlantic Ocean.

Mecox Beach, Jobs Lane, Bridgehampton; (631) 728–8585.

Town of Southampton beach with 250 feet on the Atlantic Ocean.

Looking north, a view of Jones Beach in winter

Montauk Point State Park,

Montauk Point State Parkway
east to end, Montauk;
(631) 668–5000; http://nys
parks.state.ny.us.

Montauk lighthouse, rocky shoreline. From November to May
look for harbor seals lounging on
rocks off the northern side of
Montauk Point. Surf casting (no
license), hiking trails. Watch out
for deer ticks.

Ocean Beach Park, enter

between Nevada Avenue and
Maple Boulevard, Long Beach;
(516) 431–1021; www.long
beachny.org.

City of Long Beach beach with 4
miles on the Atlantic Ocean, with
2.2-mile boardwalk.

Otis G. Pike National Wilder-
ness Area, between Watch Hill

and Smith Point, Fire Island;
(631) 281–3010; www.nps
.gov/fiis.

Visitor center at Smith Point
County Park. This is the only
federally designated wilderness
area in New York State, stretch-
ing nearly 8 miles over 1,360
acres. This expanse of high dune,
salt marshes, fresh marshes, and
beach is straddled by the Atlantic
Ocean on one side and the Great
South Bay on the other. On the
bay beach you will see green, red,
and brown algae. Hiking requires
precautions against ticks, mosquitoes, poison ivy, and sunburn.
Since there are virtually no
marked trails, the area is much as
it was before settlers arrived on
Long Island. The Long Island

Beach dunes and vegetation at Fire Island's Otis G. Pike National Wilderness Area

Seashore Trail stretches from
Watch Hill to Smith Point. Information is available at the Watch
Hill Visitor Center, reached by
ferry from Patchogue.

An aerial view of Shadmoor State Park at Ditch Plains in Montauk

Overlook Beach, Ocean Parkway, east of Cedar Beach, off Wantagh and Robert Moses Parkways, Babylon; (631) 893–2100; www .townofbabylon.com/guides.cfm.

Town of Babylon beach with three-quarters of a mile on the Atlantic Ocean.

Pikes Beach, off Dune Road, Westhampton Dunes; (631) 728–8585.

Town of Southampton beach with 400 feet on the Atlantic Ocean.

Point Lookout, Lido Boulevard, Point Lookout; (516) 431–3900; www.townofhempstead.org.

Town of Hempstead beach with 1,800 feet on the Atlantic Ocean, across inlet from Jones Beach.

Ponquogue Beach, Dune Road, Hampton Bays; (631) 728–8585.

Town of Southampton beach with 600 feet on the Atlantic Ocean.

Robert Moses State Park, Sagtikos Parkway south to Robert Moses Causeway, Fire Island; (631) 669–0470.

A 5-mile beach with four bathhouses and a nearby boat basin with pump-out and bait stations. Field 2 and field 5 are open year-round (fee on weekends and holidays). Four sand wheelchairs, fishing.

Sagg Main Beach, Sagg Main Road, Sagaponack; (631) 728–8585.

Town of Southampton beach with 1,500 feet on the Atlantic Ocean.

Sailors Haven Beach, Fire Island; (631) 589–8980 (ferry); www.nps.gov/fiis/.

Reached by Sailors Haven ferry or by private boat. Quarter- to half-mile walk from marina.

Sands Picnic Beach, 710 Lido Boulevard, Lido Beach; (516) 431–3900.

Town of Hempstead beach with 380 feet on the Atlantic Ocean.

Shadmoor State Park, Montauk Highway and Seaside Avenue, Montauk; (631) 668–5000; http://nysparks.state.ny.us.

Ocean beach, freshwater wetlands, and hiking and biking trails.

Smith Point County Park, William Floyd Parkway (Long Island Expressway, exit 68 south) to the southern terminus, Fire Island; (631) 852–1313; www.suffolkcountyny.gov.

At 2,290 acres, Suffolk's largest oceanfront park has a 5-mile protected beach, campsites, saltwater fishing, waterfowl, beach camping, and picnic areas. Off-road vehicles are allowed with permit only on the western portion of the outer beach. Beachgoers are advised to respect marked, protective fencing around the nest sites of endangered shorebirds.

Tiana Beach, off Dune Road, East Quogue; (631) 728–8585.

Town of Southampton beach with 1,000 feet on the Atlantic Ocean.

Tobay Beach, Ocean Parkway east of Jones Beach off Wantagh Parkway, Massapequa; (516) 679–3900.

Town of Oyster Bay beach with 2 miles on the Atlantic Ocean, plus some bay swimming on South Oyster Bay.

W. Scott Cameron Beach, end of Dune Road, Bridgehampton; (631) 728–8585.

Town of Southampton beach with 300 feet on the Atlantic Ocean.

Watch Hill Beach, Fire Island; (631) 475–1665 (ferry); www .nps.gov/fiis/.

Reached by Watch Hill ferry or by private boat. Quarter- to half-mile walk from marina.

On and Near Long Island Sound

Bar Beach Park, West Shore Road, off Roslyn Road, Port Washington; (516) 327–3140 or (516) 767–4625; www.northhempstead.com.

Town of North Hempstead beach with quarter-mile on Hempstead Harbor, off Long Island Sound.

Callahans Beach, end of Callahans Beach Road, off Route 25A, Fort Salonga; (631) 754–9808.

Town of Smithtown beach with 300 feet on Smithtown Bay, off Long Island Sound.

Caumsett State Historic Park, 25 Lloyd Harbor Road, Lloyd Neck; (631) 423–1770; http://nysparks.state.ny.us.

The 1,500-acre park sits at the head of a scenic peninsula jutting into Long Island Sound; 27 miles of trails, cycling allowed with helmets, scuba diving area with permit, fishing with permit, bridle trails, and nature walks.

A relaxed angler at Cedar Beach in Mount Sinai on Long Island Sound

Kayakers off Bayville's Charles E. Ransom Beach

Cedar Beach, Harbor Beach Road, Mount Sinai; (631) 451–6100; www.brookhaven.org.

Town of Brookhaven beach with 3,450 feet on Long Island Sound.

Centerport Beach, off Little Neck Road, Centerport; (631) 261–7574.

Town of Huntington beach with 230 feet on Northport Bay, off the Sound.

Centre Island Beaches, off Bayville–Centre Island Road, Bayville; (516) 624–6124.

Town of Oyster Bay beaches with 350 feet on Oyster Bay Harbor, 650 feet on Long Island Sound.

Charles E. Ransom Beach, Bayville Avenue, Bayville; (516) 624–6160.

Town of Oyster Bay beach with 800 feet on Long Island Sound.

Crab Meadow Beach, end of Waterside Avenue, Northport; (631) 261–7574.

Town of Huntington beach with 1,060 feet on Long Island Sound.

Crescent Beach, end of Crescent Beach Road, off Landing Road, Glen Cove; (516) 676–3766; www.glencove-li.com.

City of Glen Cove beach with 75 feet on Long Island Sound.

Goldsmith's Inlet County Park, off Mill Road, Peconic; (631) 854–4949; www.suffolkcountyny.gov.

Features sixty acres, good bird-watching. A half-mile hiking trail leads to Long Island Sound. Lim-ited parking off Soundview Avenue.

Gov. Alfred E. Smith/Sunken Meadow State Park, north end of Sunken Meadow State Park-way, Kings Park; (631) 269–4333.

Three-mile beach on Long Island Sound, beach ramp, and fishing (for permit and season informa-tion, call 631–669–1000).

Inlet Pond County Preserve, Main Road access off Route 48, Greenport; (631) 854–4949; www.suffolkcountyny.gov.

North Fork Audubon Society and Town of Southold maintain this site with Suffolk County. Fea-tures thirty-nine acres on Long Island Sound, surf-fishing. No parking near preserve.

Iron Pier Beach, end of Pier Avenue, off Sound Avenue, Aquebogue; (631) 727–5744; www.riverheadli.com.

Town of Riverhead beach with 480 feet on Long Island Sound.

Long Beach, Long Beach Road, off Moriches Road, Nissequogue; (631) 584–9683.

Town of Smithtown beach with 300 feet on Smithtown Bay off Long Island Sound.

Morgan Memorial Park Beach, Germaine Street at the end of Landing Road, Glen Cove; (516) 676–3766; www.glencove-li.com.

City of Glen Cove beach with 350 feet on Hempstead Harbor.

Orient Point County Park, end of Route 25 near the Orient Point ferry, Orient; (631) 854–4949; www.suffolkcountyny.gov.

Features forty-eight acres, a mile-long beach, a half-mile hiking trail, bird-watching, and views of Long Island Sound.

Pryibil Beach, at end of East Beach Road, off Lattingtown Road; (516) 676–3766; www.glencove-li.com.

City of Glen Cove beach with 500 feet of beachfront on Long Island Sound.

Reeves Park Beach, end of Park Road, off Sound Avenue, Aquebogue; (631) 727–5744; www.riverheadli.com.

Town of Riverhead beach with 240 feet on Long Island Sound.

Shoreham Beach, North Country Road, Shoreham; (631) 451–6100; www.brookhaven.org.

Town of Brookhaven beach with 600 feet on Long Island Sound.

Short Beach, off Boney Lane from Moriches and Long Beach Roads, Nissequogue; (631) 360–7654.

Town of Smithtown beach with 300 feet on Smithtown Bay, off Long Island Sound.

Southold Town Beach, on Route 48, Southold; (631) 765–5182.

Beach has 960 feet on Long Island Sound.

Stony Brook Beach, Sand Street, Stony Brook; (631) 451–6100; www.brookhaven.org.

Town of Brookhaven beach with 225 feet on Long Island Sound.

Theodore Roosevelt County Park, 3 miles east of Montauk Village on Montauk Highway; (631) 852–7878; www.co .suffolk.ny.us.

A father and son fish with a seine at Sunken Meadow State Park in Kings Park

The end of a July day at West Meadow Beach in Stony Brook

Features 1,126 acres, 3.5 miles of nature trails, waterfowl and deer, 5 miles of bridle paths with rentals, outer beach camping (off-road vehicle permit needed), freshwater fishing, and unprotected beach. Outer beach access at East Lake Drive.

Wading River Beach, Creek Road, off North Wading River and Sound Roads, Wading River; (631) 727–5744.

Town of Riverhead beach with 250 feet on Long Island Sound.

West Meadow Beach, West Meadow Beach Road, Stony Brook; (631) 451–6100.

Town of Brookhaven beach with 1,100 feet on Long Island Sound.

West Neck Beach, off West Neck Road, Lloyd Harbor; (631) 261–7574.

Town of Huntington beach with 1,140 feet on Cold Spring Harbor, off Long Island Sound.

Wildwood State Park, North Wading River Road, off Sound Avenue, north on Hulse Landing Road, Wading River; (631) 929–4314.

This 769-acre park sits above a rugged stretch of shoreline on Long Island Sound, with hiking trails and saltwater fishing.

Excursions

Atlantis Marine World, 431 East Main Street, Riverhead; (631) 208–9200; www.atlantismarineworld.com.

Watch sea creatures in marine habitats at this year-round aquarium and education center on the Peconic River. Environmental boat tours and simulated submarine rides are available.

Coastal Research and Education Society of Long Island, Dowling College, Idle Hour Boulevard, Oakdale; (631) 244–3352; www.cresli.org.

Offers offshore cruises, some as long as thirty-six hours. Join scientists to find, photograph, and collect information about whales, sea turtles, and pelagic birds.

The **Moonchaser,** Captree State Park, Babylon; (631) 661–5061.

Among its activities are sightseeing cruises Tuesday through Friday and Sunday at 1:00 P.M. from May through October. Call to confirm.

Nautical Princess, Freeport; (516) 623–5712; www.nautical-cruiselines.com.

Among other activities, it offers seal-watching.

Riverhead Foundation for Marine Research and Preservation, 467 East Main Street, Riverhead; (631) 369–9840; www.riverheadfoundation.org.

Located at Atlantis Marine World and dedicated to protecting the environment, the foundation operates harbor seal observation walks from Montauk from December through April, as well as seal cruises from Point Lookout in Nassau County from January through March.

Scuba diving

Broadway Divers, 490 Sunrise Highway, Rockville Centre; (516) 872–4571; www.swimand scuba.com.

Wreck, beach, and Wednesday-night dives April to December; trips; rafting. Meets 8:00 P.M. the second Tuesday of the month.

Dive Club, P.O. Box 96, West Islip 11795; (631) 321–4707; www.thediveclub.com.

Trips and instruction.

Long Island Divers Association, (631) 327–8924; www.lida online.com.

Works with public parks to obtain beach access for divers. Meets the third Wednesday of the month at Suffolk County Sports Hall of Fame, 62 South Ocean Avenue, Patchogue.

Long Island Dolphins, P.O. Box 888, Miller Place 11764; (516) 818–1115; www.garloo.org.

Two weekly wreck dives April to November. Meets monthly begin-

Sharks at Atlantis Marine World in Riverhead

ning in April aboard *Garloo*, docked at Captree State Park boat basin, east end of Ocean Parkway, Babylon.

Long Island Groupers, 2731 Hempstead Turnpike, Levittown; (516) 796–6560; www.tdconline .com.

Group has local beach and wreck dives, six beginner trips yearly, and a scuba club for adults.

Nassau County parks dive sites include: Bay Park, western side of the park, visibility of 5 to 8 feet, First Avenue, East Rockaway, (516) 571–7821; Garvies Point Museum and Preserve, maximum depth 18 feet, Barry Drive, Glen Cove, (516) 571–8010; Hempstead Harbor Beach Park, recommended for novice divers, gear checks and training purposes, easy water entry, maximum depth 16 feet, visibility 6 feet, West Shore Road, Port Washington, (516) 571–7930; Inwood Park, north side of park, entry from shore, gradual slope to a maximum depth of 23 to 25 feet 20 yards offshore, acceptable for training, foot of Bayview Avenue, Inwood, (516) 571–7894. Call sites for availability; diving by permit only. Obtain permits at the parks administration building at Eisenhower Park, Hempstead Turnpike, East Meadow, weekdays 10:00 A.M. to 4:00 P.M.; applicants must have a county leisure pass and diver's certification card. For details call (516) 572–0230.

A minke whale near Cape Cod, Massachusetts, as seen during a long-distance cruise from Long Island sponsored by the Coastal Research and Education Society

Sea Searchers, (631) 786–1286; www.groups.yahoo.com/group/sea searchers.

Two local dives a month, newsletter. Meets at Suffolk County Sports Hall of Fame, 62 South Ocean Avenue, Patchogue, on the second Thursday of the month.

Seahunt Divers Team, (516) 398–2838; www.kirbyscorner.net.

Trips and instruction.

SeaScapes USA, 317 Jackson Avenue, Syosset; (516) 433–7757; www.seascapesusa.com.

Wreck, beach, night, and ice diving; out-of-state trips; weekend social events; and monthly meetings.

Suffolk County parks allow diving in these parks: Cedar Point County Park, East Hampton (novices dive in Northwest Harbor west of the park, intermediate level in Gardiner's Bay north of the park, and more advanced at Cedar Point Lighthouse just offshore); Theodore Roosevelt County Park, Montauk (novice to intermediate, outer beach, accessible by four-wheel-drive vehicles); Smith Point County Park, Shirley (intermediate to advanced at slack tide); Cupsogue Beach County Park, Westhampton (intermediate to advanced at slack tide); Meschutt Beach County Park, Hampton Bays (snorkeling along the jetty). Call (631) 854–4949 for details.

Dive boats

Eagles Nest, Town of Hempstead East Marina, Lido Boulevard, Point Lookout; (516) 897–9157; www.eaglesnestwreck diving.com.

Capacity: 8 divers for overnight trips; 24 divers on day trips. Luxury dive boats, shipwreck diving.

Hampton Dive Center, 369 Route 24, Riverhead; (631) 727–7578; www.hampton dive.com.

Lessons, equipment rental, and excursions, including shark diving.

***Jean Marie* Dive Charters,** Jackson's Marina, 6 Teepee Street, Hampton Bays; (631) 728–5168; www.jeanmariedivecharters.com.

Capacity: 15. Night and weekend dives, custom dives.

Point Break, Unique Charters, P.O. Box 824, Shoreham 11786; (631) 821–3483; www.unique charters.com.

Capacity: 6. Sails out of Greenport, Port Jefferson, and the Moriches. Wreck, reef, lobster and bottle diving; salvage; customized diving.

Research Vessel *Garloo,* Captree State Park boat basin, east end of Ocean Parkway, Babylon; (845) 735–5550; www.garloo.org.

Scuba diving and trips.

Research Vessel *Wreck Valley,* Jones Inlet, Baldwin; (516) 868–2658; www.aquaexplorers.com.

Capacity: 6.

Sea Hawk, 578 Guy Lombardo Avenue, Woodcleft Canal, Freeport; (718) 279–1345.

Capacity: 10.

Sea Hunter III, 11 Hudson Avenue, Freeport; (516) 735–8308.

Capacity: 30. Wreck diving.

Shell Collecting

Long Island Shell Club, (516) 785–8211.

The club hosts occasional meetings and outings.

Divers on a November day in Hempstead Harbor at Garvies Point Museum and Preserve

A great egret on the Carmans River in the Wertheim National Wildlife Refuge in Shirley

The Rivers and Bays

By Joe Haberstroh

In the sun-washed loneliness of Hallock Bay, far out on Long Island's North Fork, commercial clammers still rake for shellfish. Farther west kayakers paddle past egrets stilt-legged in the shallows of the lower Carmans River. In Nassau County suburban anglers roost on the steel fishing bridge that spans Massapequa Creek.

If the wide-open ocean somehow belongs to everyone—visitors included—Long Island's rivers, bays, ponds, and streams have a distinctly local and even intimate atmosphere. From only a few miles out on the ocean, this Island is a smudge on the horizon. But the rivers and bays take us deep into the interior, past backyards and fishing docks and to places where even now there is not a single house.

Measuring a brook trout, Long Island's only native trout, for a study before returning it to the Carmans River

The bays give Long Island its shape, its stony cuts and sandy curves. The Peconic Estuary alone includes more than one hundred distinct bays, harbors, and tributaries. The freshwater profile is equally diverse, even if the bodies of water are modest. The Peconic River, the mightiest of the Island's four rivers, is only 12 miles long. The Island's largest of more than sixty significant lakes and ponds, Lake Ronkonkoma, is only 243 acres.

There is a sturdy, flat-bottomed boat made locally—a garvey—that is typical of the sort of craft needed to fish in these waters. Something with which to nose into

Sunrise Highway traffic next to the Connetquot River State Park Preserve, once a hunting club

the shallows, where fish often dwell among the submerged stands of eel grass. On the bays, depending on the season, anglers can dream of hard tugs on the line—a striped bass perhaps, bluefish, and weakfish. A hardware-store crab trap dropped into the water from the docks at Captree State Park, on the South Shore, can reliably yield a dinner, and it pays to be handy with a clam rake at low tide in places such as Bellport Bay.

In the interior, what anglers call "light tackle" will do. Here are small- and largemouth bass, carp, brown trout, and, just for beginners, blue gill. The luckiest at streamside might

A ring-billed gull on the
Nissequogue River

Slider turtles on the Carmans River in Shirley

land a brook trout—Long Island's only native trout—a fish that is famously wily and savory
and striped in the vivid red of an early autumn sunset.

Long Island's rivers are less for anglers. They exist more for the paddler, the hiker, the
lover of frogs and turtles and salamanders. (Long Island has eight types of salamanders.)
The rivers are a single hydrological rung above streams: The Carmans covers about 10
miles; the Connetquot, 8; the Nissequogue, 8; and the longest of the four, the Peconic,
measures 12 miles. Some can be forded with a briefly considered leap. Their courses

The Peconic River in Riverhead, looking south

meander under varied canopies of pitch pine, white oak, black walnut, red maple, chestnut, and weeping birch. In autumn the Carmans is especially alive with the exuberance of maples showing their color before they drift off to their winter rest.

And the Peconic in particular is a stream of startling contrasts. It starts in a thick woods and is so shallow that a canoe scrapes more than glides. It ends farther east, where it opens into the Peconic Bay and where the power of the ocean can be sensed in the surging tides and briny breeze.

These local waters may seem like pale diversions when compared to the violent Atlantic and to the quieter majesty of the Sound. In fact these rivers, bays, ponds, and streams run deep into the heart of Long Island.

Alewives

What: Each spring these herringlike fish swim from points far offshore and up the Peconic River with the aid of a fish ladder—a chute bolted into place at the spillway in Riverhead's Grangebel Park. Local conservationists envision a series of ladders that would allow the alewives to bypass several dams and return to their ancient breeding grounds upriver.

When: In time with the alewives' spring "run," the ladder is installed March 1 and removed May 1.

Where: The park is just west of Main Street and Peconic Avenue.

Keep in Mind: The top of the ladder is enclosed. With great variability, the fish can be seen emerging from the high end of the ladder each day about two hours before low tide.

An alewife from the Peconic in Riverhead

Installing a fish ladder at Grangebel Park in Riverhead to enable alewives to reach breeding grounds up the Peconic River

Eastern Tiger Salamander

What: The biggest of Long Island's mole salamanders, these yellow pond-breeders have dark tabby bands and live nowhere else in New York State. Here, they grow up to 8 inches long.

When: They spend most of their life buried in leaves on the forest floor, but in early spring when rains and rising temperatures start to thaw iced-over ponds, Eastern tiger salamanders creep out by night and return to the pools of their births to mate and lay eggs.

Where: Seasonal ponds in the pine barrens around Manorville and east. The South Fork Natural History Society offers a nocturnal Eastern tiger salamander hunt in Bridgehampton during mating season; call (631) 537–9735 for times.

Keep in Mind: They're endangered in New York State; try not to disturb them or their habitat.

Long Island's Eastern tiger salamander, found nowhere else in New York State

Snapping Turtles

What: Long Island's largest common turtles, snappers can inhabit any permanent body of freshwater. Although more placid in the water, where they often remain buried in mud with just their eyes showing, the turtles tend to turn ornery on land. Nevertheless, their prehistoric-looking tail, graceful glides in the water, and lumbering movements when ashore make them fascinating to watch—from a distance.

When: They emerge to lay their Ping Pong ball–size eggs in late May and June; hatchlings can appear through October. The turtles often laze in the sunshine during the day before they become more active at night.

Where: Head to Long Island's midsize ponds. Some even inhabit brackish water—found in streams leading from ponds to the South Shore bays, for instance. Heftier specimens can be found in Quogue Wildlife Refuge, Caleb Smith State Park, and the Wertheim National Wildlife Refuge (on logs lodged along the Carmans River).

Keep in Mind: They bite. Look, but do not touch.

Zoologist Peter Warny with a pair of small snappers at Caleb Smith State Park Preserve in Smithtown

Tropical Fish

What: Fish from tropical waters appear each summer in South Shore waters, especially Shinnecock Bay. The visitors include spotfish, butterflyfish, triggerfish, lionfish, and angelfish. All but the larger fish, which can swim back south, die off in the fall when the waters around Long Island get too cold for them.

When: Late August into fall.

Where: Near the old Ponquogue Bridge in Hampton Bays (across from Dune Road, a bit west of the Shinnecock Inlet); around Fire Island Inlet; also in the shallows along Montauk Highway, just east of the Shinnecock Canal.

Keep in Mind: Scuba diving is the best way to see the fish. Keep track of tides and currents and don't touch any fish. Some, such as triggerfish, will bite; others, such as lionfish, are poisonous.

A colorful angelfish caught in Shinnecock Bay, thousands of miles from its home in the tropics

The Carmans River, at top left, through the Wertheim National Wildlife Refuge; Big Fish Creek runs through the center

Wertheim National Wildlife Refuge

What: The 2,550-acre complex bisected by the scenic Carmans River boasts a bounty of wildlife and one of the last undeveloped estuary systems on Long Island. More than 240 bird species have been documented here, including ospreys, great blue herons, peregrine falcons, and the largest breeding population of wood ducks of any park on the Island. Irises, marsh buttercups, and violets grace the refuge in the spring, while vibrant red, orange, and yellow leaves decorate its upland forests in the fall, providing a spectacular backdrop to 4 miles of hiking trails and some of the best canoeing on the Island.

When: The refuge is open every day, 8:00 A.M. to 4:30 P.M., and offers excellent opportunities to commune with nature year-round.
Where: Smith Road off Montauk Highway, Shirley.
Keep in Mind: Trail maps are available at the refuge's main office. For details call (631) 286–0485. As residents of a wildlife refuge, all of the flora and fauna here are protected. While you can stop and smell the buttercups, please don't pick them.

The Carmans

River: Carmans (CAR-mens), named for a former landowner, Samuel Carman.

Length: About 10 miles, Long Island's second-longest river.

Route: Considered the region's most pristine river, the cold Carmans begins as a freshwater spring near Route 25. It passes through federal and county land from Yaphank, where it widens, and then empties into the Great South Bay. The Carmans flows from north to south, typical for South Shore streams.

Widest point: The mouth, in the Wertheim National Wildlife Refuge, is about 800 yards wide.

Deepest point: Also the mouth.

Current speed: Varies; usually gentle.

Fish: Largemouth bass, panfish, bluegill, and sunfish. Stocked fish include rainbow and brown trout.

Wildlife: American osprey, belted kingfisher, canvasback duck, American wigeon, mallard, bald eagle, great blue heron, songbird, bat, red fox, white-tailed deer, wild turkey, muskrat, and river otter.

Plants: The sour gum tree displays vibrant fall hues. There's also wild watercress, pokeweed, wintergreen, tupelo, skunk cabbage, sassafras, black walnut, white oak, and pitch pine.

Activities: Kayaking and canoeing on the lower portion; fishing and hiking along entire river.

History: By the 1700s settlers had nearly eradicated Native Americans, who once ate the river's clams and used the shells as currency. More than a decade later, Samuel Carman ran a river-powered mill and built a house with a post office, store, and tavern. In the 1920s duck hunting and pleasure sailing flourished; sailing could only be done on the tidal section south of Montauk Highway.

Unusual fact: The river was first known as the Connecticut River, an Indian word for "at the long river."

Canoeists on the Carmans in Shirley, framed by a railroad bridge

The Carmans in late fall

The Connetquot

River: Connetquot (Kah-NET-quott), Indian for "at the long river." (*Connecticut* is a variation.)

Length: About 8 miles.

Route: Originating as a spring seepage just south of the Ronkonkoma Moraine in Lakeland County Park in Islandia, the river flows south through Connetquot River State Park Preserve in Oakdale. At the park's southern end, the river flows into Main Pond, just north of the Sunrise Highway. South of the highway, the river widens, becomes an estuary, and empties into the Great South Bay.

Widest point: About 275 yards wide, in Main Pond.

Deepest point: About 7½ feet, also in Main Pond.

Current speed: Approximately 2 to 3 mph. South of Sunrise Highway its direction changes with the tides. Dams above keep it flowing south.

Fish: Native fish are the brook trout, blacknose dace, pirate perch, and bluegill sunfish. Stocked fish include rainbow and brown trout.

Wildlife: Heron, egret, raccoon, fox, chipmunk, rabbit, swan, osprey, deer, eastern bluebird, and yellowthroat warbler.

Plants: Pitch pine and white oak in sandy soil. Rarities include Pyxie moss and small orchids.

A placid Connetquot in Oakdale

Activities: Fishing, bird-watching, hiking, and horseback riding. Boat launching is prohibited in the park.

History: Wealthy sportsmen and other notables, including President Ulysses S. Grant and General William Tecumseh Sherman, used the river as a private trout stream and hunting preserve for more than a century. It opened to the public in 1978.

Unusual fact: The largest fish caught was a rainbow trout weighing nineteen pounds, eight ounces.

The Connetquot River in a view looking west

The Nissequogue

River: Nissequogue (NIS-suh-quogg), name is derived from the Nesaquake Indians.

Length: Roughly 8 miles.

Route: A tidal river, it begins as small springs in Hauppauge. It flows north through Blydenburgh County Park and Caleb Smith State Park Preserve, where it becomes a swiftly moving trout stream. After it crosses Route 25, the river mixes with saltwater and begins to widen. It empties into Smithtown Bay and Long Island Sound, passing through several more parks.

Widest point: Just north of San Remo.

Deepest point: In boating channel from Old Dock Road boat ramp in Kings Park into Smithtown Bay. (Six feet deep at mean low water.)

Current speed: Can reach about 2 mph. Check tide charts; go with the flow.

Fish: The native fish is the brook trout. The river is stocked with brook, brown, and rainbow trout weekly from April to mid-October.

Wildlife: The river flows through a section of Nissequogue River State Park, close to Smithtown Bay, a spot designated as a state bird conservation area, drawing osprey, snowy egret, and great horned owl.

Plants: Chestnut tree, weeping birch, and tupelo.

Activities: Access is limited, but there are numerous education programs. Fishing is permitted, but boat access is prohibited north of Route 25. There is canoe and kayak access at Route 25 and at Nissequogue River State Park.

History: Land was given to Englishman Lion Gardiner by the Montaukett Indians, grateful for Gardiner's role in rescuing the chieftain's daughter from another tribe in 1663. In the late nineteenth century, the railroad and improved roads reduced river traffic. In 1963 the state purchased the property and it later became Caleb Smith State Park.

Unusual fact: Because of its origin the river is actually a spring creek, a stream that flows from groundwater with a constant flow and temperature.

Short Beach in Kings Park at the mouth of the Nissequogue

The Nissequogue River meandering through wetlands toward Long Island Sound

The Peconic

River: Peconic (Puh-CON-nick), translated by some as the Indian word for "calm."

Length: Long Island's longest river flows about 12 miles.

Route: Originating in a small depression on the west side of the William Floyd Parkway adjacent to the Brookhaven National Laboratory, the Peconic meanders eastward and then empties into Flanders Bay, which flows into Peconic Bay.

Widest point: Forge Pond, also known as Peconic Lake; just west of Riverhead.

Deepest point: A 6- to 8-foot navigational channel dredged from downtown Riverhead to Flanders Bay.

Current speed: Roughly 2 mph.

Fish: The Peconic is home to snapper bluefish, the endangered banded sunfish, American eel, yellow perch, largemouth bass, alewife, brown bullhead (catfish), carp, and two types of pickerel—chain and red fin.

Wildlife: Birds include the great blue heron, kingfisher, and cliff and bank swallow. Hummingbirds have been spotted here. Deer, muskrat, and mink are visible.

Plants: Honeysuckle, poison ivy, poison sumac, button bush, cattail, swamp maple, red maple, pitch pine, and white oak.

Activities: Freshwater fishing, canoeing, kayaking, and nature-watching. Hand-carry boats permitted.

History: Early English settlers discovered iron ore in the river, and in the mid-1700s constructed an iron forge. Cranberry bogs were later cultivated. The businesses are all but gone, but the crimson berries still grow randomly.

Unusual fact: It's the only river that flows from west to east across the Island.

A kayaker on the Peconic in Riverhead

In Riverhead, the mouth of the Peconic, Long Island's only eastward-flowing river

Life of a Clam

Hard clams *(Mercenaria mercenaria)* lead lives of quiet sedentariness. Poets have found little inspiration in clams.

And yet, the hard clam is arguably the most celebrated marine organism of Long Island.

Although their numbers have long been in decline, clams helped build Long Island's original communities, fill stomachs, and provide jobs.

These are self-contained eating and reproduction machines. Their shells, banded with raised concentric growth rings, are chocolate brown to bone-white. Inside, the shell is purple. Consumers buy them by familiar names: littlenecks (which measure 2 to 3 inches across the hinge), cherrystones (3 to 4 inches), and chowders (the least valuable at 4 inches and larger). In the middle of the twentieth century, the Great South Bay claimed almost two-thirds of the nation's clam production. Female clams release on average eight million eggs over a spring and summer. Within ten hours of the egg being released and fertilized, the clam is feeding.

Within twenty-four hours it has a shell. The clams settle to the bottom after two weeks.

Clams take three years to achieve full size. As adults, they are buried in the sand, except for their siphon, which extends into the water above. Clams eat by pumping water through their siphon, selecting the animal or plant particles that are small enough for them to digest, then pumping the water back out.

When they are seed size, clams are defenseless against predators—especially fish. Even when they are larger, they can be plucked from the sand by crabs. Clams dig deeper into the sand when threatened. It's unclear how much or how frequently adult clams move, though clam "tracks" are spotted on bay bottoms around Long Island. Generally they are safely embedded in the sand, with an anchoring appendage called a foot often hanging below them, and their siphon reaching through the substrate above.

Suspended in this way, clams are immune to most attacks from natural predators. A mature clam's abductor muscle keeps the animal's twin shells firmly shut. Armored this way, and hidden, clams can live up to fifty years. But that's not why they are happy. The phrase "happy as a clam at high tide" makes sense. At high tide, they are covered in water and hidden from clam-diggers.

—JOE HABERSTROH

ON THE RIVERS AND BAYS

By Laura Mann

Although it is surrounded by ocean and sound, Long Island is also defined by dozens of rivers, bays, harbors, and ponds. Here is a selection of these bodies of water. Access to many municipal beaches is restricted. Call ahead for details.

Bellows Pond

Sears Bellows County Park, Bellows Pond Road, Flanders; (631) 852–8290; www.co.suffolk.ny.us.

Two hundred feet of pond beachfront; park has 693 acres with fishing, hunting, and boat rentals.

Big Fresh Pond

Emma Rose Elliston Park, Millstone Road, off North Sea Road, North Sea; (631) 728–8585.

Town of Southampton beach with 150 feet on Big Fresh Pond.

Carmans River

Southaven County Park, Victory Avenue, off William Floyd Parkway, Brookhaven; (631) 854–1414; www.co.suffolk.ny.us.

The park has more than 1,300 acres, with trails through woods and along the Carmans River. Brook trout, rainbow trout, and largemouth bass are prevalent.

Wertheim National Wildlife Refuge, 300 Smith Road, Shirley; (631) 286–0485; http://refuges.fws.gov.

The lower Carmans River runs through this 2,550-acre refuge. For more detail see "On the Trails" in Chapter 2.

Connetquot River

Bayard Cutting Arboretum State Park, Southern State Parkway,

Wild turkeys at the Connetquot River State Park Preserve

exit 45E (Montauk Highway), east three-quarters of a mile to Arboretum, Great River; (631) 581–1002; http://nysparks.state .ny.us.

The 690-acre former estate of William Bayard Cutting is nestled in an idyllic setting on the Connetquot River as it flows into the Great South Bay. Five marked nature walks pass wildflowers, pinetum, marshes, meadows, and the river's shores. Tours by appointment only.

Connetquot River State Park Preserve, Sunrise Highway, exit 47A (accessible from westbound lanes only), Oakdale; (631) 581–1005; http://nysparks.state.ny.us.

Free permit required. Has 3,473 acres of woods, fields, ponds, creeks, and river, with more than 33 miles of marked and unmarked trails. The unspoiled Connetquot River is visited by a variety of wildfowl and is stocked with brook, rainbow, and brown trout.

Fall colors at Connetquot River State Park Preserve

Lakeland County Park, Johnson Avenue, Islandia; (631) 853–2727; www.suffolkcountyny.gov.

Features seventy acres; nature trail boardwalk over Connetquot River; self-guided interpretive sensory trails; tactile maps for the visually impaired; and nature trails, fishing, recreation, and picnicking.

Gardiners Bay

Cedar Point County Park, Stephen Hands Path, East Hampton; (631) 852–7620; www.suffolkcountyny.gov.

Features 608 acres on Gardiners Bay, campsites, nature trail, fishing with permit, waterfowl, rowboat rentals, and picnic area.

A path to the Great South Bay at Gardiner County Park in West Bay Shore

Maidstone Park, end of Flaggy Hole Road, off Three Mile Harbor Road and Hog Creek Highway, East Hampton; (631) 324–2417.

Town of East Hampton beach with 400 feet on Gardiners Bay.

Northwest Harbor County Park, off Swamp Road, East Hampton; (631) 854–4949; www.suffolk countyny.gov.

Features 337 acres on a salt marsh, migratory waterfowl, deer; on Northwest Harbor near Gardiners Bay

Orient Beach State Park, east end of North Country Road (Route 25), Orient; (631) 323–2440.

Ten miles of beachfront including wilderness areas for shell collecting, plant study, and birdwatching. Has a 300-foot beach on Gardiners Bay, two sand wheelchairs, hiking, Roy Latham Maritime Forest Trail, Long Beach Trail with self-guided brochures or scheduled guided tours.

Great South Bay

Atlantique Beach and Marina, end of Atlantic Avenue, Fire Island; (631) 583–8610.

Town of Islip beach with halfmile on the Atlantic Ocean and a smaller beach on Great South Bay.

Captree State Park, off Robert Moses Causeway at end of Sagtikos Parkway, Babylon; (631) 669–0449; http://nysparks.state .ny.us.

Captree's 298 acres focus on a boat basin off the New York State Boat Channel on the north side of the park.

Corey Beach, Corey Avenue, Blue Point; (631) 451–6100; www.brookhaven.org.

Town of Brookhaven beach with 500 feet on Great South Bay.

Fire Island National Seashore, accessible by private boat and ferries; (631) 289–4810; www.nps.gov/fiis.

Fire Island, a 32-mile-long barrier beach, separates the Atlantic Ocean from the Great South Bay. Twenty-six miles of the island have been designated a national seashore, which includes extensive areas of the Great South Bay, Narrows Bay, and Moriches Bay. The variety of wildlife on the island is astounding. Beach and bayside have fiddler and horseshoe crabs, blue crabs, shellfish, and various snails. More than forty species of fish have been collected from the Great South Bay, including bluefish, striped bass, mackerel, and weakfish. The Sailors Haven and Watch Hill areas are usually open May 15 to October 15. The Fire Island Light Station, William Floyd Estate, and the Fire Island Wilderness visitor center (Smith Point) are accessible year-round, but operating hours vary. (Also see Otis G. Pike National Wilderness Area in Chapter 3.)

Gardiner County Park, Montauk Highway, a half-mile east of the Robert Moses Causeway, West

A view of the vast Great South Bay from the shore of Heckscher State Park in East Islip

Bay Shore; (631) 854–0935 (seasonally) or (631) 854–4949; www.co.suffolk.ny.us.

The 231-acre park on the Great South Bay has 3.5 miles of wide trails. The main trail, Beach Road, leads from the parking lot to the bay, where the vista is spectacular. To your east are salt marsh and osprey towers, and across the bay to your left is the Fire Island Lighthouse. From here you can see Robert Moses State Park and Captree Island.

Heckscher State Park, at the end of Heckscher State Parkway, East Islip; (631) 581–2100; http://nysparks.state.ny.us.

Black ducks in the marshes at the William Floyd Estate at Mastic Beach

The park offers 20 miles of trails with 1,657 acres of woods, marsh beach, and dune, including 1.2 miles of beachfront on Great South Bay.

Islip Beach, South Bay Avenue south of Sunrise Highway, Islip; (631) 224–5345.

Town of Islip beach with 300 yards on Great South Bay.

John F. Kennedy Memorial Wildlife Sanctuary, Tobay Beach, east of Jones Beach, Massapequa; (516) 797–4110; free permit required from Town of Oyster Bay Department of Parks.

Also known as Tobay Sanctuary, this 550-acre tidal marsh contains a diversity of barrier beach habitats unusual in Nassau County. Use your binoculars to explore the variety of wildlife, including a colony of diamondback terrapins. Trails lead past birding areas, a pond, and Zachs Bay and High Hill Beach.

Sandspit Beach, Brightwood Street, Patchogue; (631) 451–6100; www.brookhaven.org.

Town of Brookhaven beach with 200 feet on Great South Bay.

Shirley Beach, Westminster and Grandview Drives, Shirley; (631) 451–6100; www.brookhaven.org.

Town of Brookhaven beach with 500 feet on Great South Bay.

Smith Point County Park, William Floyd Parkway, Shirley; (631) 852–1316; www.suffolkcountyny.gov.

Five miles on Great South Bay.

Tanner Park, Wilson Avenue off Montauk Highway, Copiague; (631) 842–7773; www.townof babylon.com/guides.cfm.

Town of Babylon beach with 300 feet on Great South Bay.

William Floyd Estate, 245 Park Drive, off William Floyd Parkway, Mastic Beach; (631) 399–2030; www.nps.gov/fiis.

The 613-acre estate is part of the Fire Island National Seashore, but is located on the mainland of Long Island. Take self-guided tours along fields, woods, ponds, and salt marsh bordering Moriches Bay.

Venetian Shores, Granada Parkway off Montauk Highway, Lindenhurst; (631) 957–1911; www.townofbabylon.com/guides.cfm.

Town of Babylon park with 1,200 feet on Great South Bay.

Greenport Harbor

Norman Klipp Park, end of Manhasset Avenue, off Route 25, Greenport; (631) 765–5182.

Town of Southold beach with 728 feet on Greenport Harbor.

Hempstead Harbor

Hempstead Harbor Beach Park, West Shore Drive, Port Washington; (516) 571–7930, (516) 571–8113 (off-season); www.co.nassau.ny.us.

Nassau County beach with half-mile on Hempstead Harbor.

Morgan Memorial Park Beach, on Germaine Street, at end of Landing Road, Glen Cove; (516) 676–3766; www.glencove-li.com.

City of Glen Cove beach with 350 feet of beachfront on Hempstead Harbor.

Hewlett Bay

Hewlett Point Park, 130 Hewlett Point Avenue, Bay Park; (516) 599–4066; www.townofhempstead.org.

Town of Hempstead beach with 1,100 feet on Hewlett Bay.

Huntington Bay

Gold Star Battalion Beach, off West Shore Road, Huntington; (631) 261–7574.

Town of Huntington beach with 400 feet on Huntington Bay.

Hobart Beach, off Asharoken Avenue, Eatons Neck; (631) 261–7574.

Town of Huntington beach with 1,725 feet on Huntington Bay.

Lake Ronkonkoma

Lake Ronkonkoma Beach, Lake Shore Road, Lake Ronkonkoma; (631) 451–6100; www.brookhaven.org.

Town of Brookhaven beach with 500 feet on lake.

Lake Ronkonkoma County Park, Lake Shore Road, Lake Ronkonkoma; (631) 854–9699; www.suffolkcountyny.gov.

On 223 acres, recreation, freshwater fishing.

Ronkonkoma Beach, Rosevale Avenue at the end of Motor Parkway, Lake Ronkonkoma; (631) 467–3308.

Town of Islip beach with 350 yards on lake.

Napeague Bay

Big Albert's Landing Beach, end of Albert's Landing Road, off Old Stone Highway, Amagansett; (631) 324–2417.

Town of East Hampton beach with 300 feet on Napeague Bay.

Nissequogue River

Arthur Kunz County Park, off Landing Avenue, Smithtown; (631) 854–4949; www.suffolkcountyny.gov.

The Long Island Greenbelt Trail moves through this ninety-seven-

Huntington's Gold Star Battalion Beach on a winter's day

Islip's portion of Ronkonkoma Beach at Long Island's largest kettle-hole lake

Theodore Roosevelt Memorial Park and Beach, Bayside Avenue, Oyster Bay; (516) 624–6202; www.oysterbaytown.com.

Town of Oyster Bay beach on harbor.

Peconic Bay and River

Foster Memorial Beach, Long Beach Road, Sag Harbor; (631) 728–8585.

Town of Southampton beach with 1 mile on Peconic Bay.

acre park with views of the Nissequogue River valley.

Nissequogue River State Park, St. Johnland Road, Kings Park; (631) 269–4927; http://nysparks .state.ny.us.

This park has 153 acres along the Nissequogue River. Hike part of the Long Island Greenbelt Trail and see the river and Long Island Sound from bluffs.

Smithtown Greenbelt County Park, off Route 347 at Nissequogue River, Smithtown; (631) 854–4949; www.suffolkcounty ny.gov.

Features 118 acres and part of the Long Island Greenbelt Trail.

Northport Bay

Asharoken Beach, Asharoken Avenue, Asharoken; (631) 261–7574.

Town of Huntington beach with 535 feet on Northport Bay.

Centerport Beach, off Little Neck Road, Centerport; (631) 261–7574.

Town of Huntington beach with 230 feet on Northport Bay, off Long Island Sound.

Crescent Beach, off Shore Drive, Huntington; (631) 261–7574.

Town of Huntington beach with 400 feet on Northport Bay.

Fleets Cove Beach, off Fleets Cove Road, Huntington; (631) 261–7574.

Town of Huntington beach with 1,600 feet of beach on Northport Bay.

Oyster Bay Harbor

Centre Island Beaches, off Bayville–Centre Island Road, Bayville; (516) 624–6124.

Town of Oyster Bay beaches with 350 feet on Oyster Bay Harbor, 650 feet on Long Island Sound.

Bluffs along the Nissequogue River, and Smithtown Bay beyond, in Kings Park

Indian Island County Park, Cross River Drive (Route 105), Riverhead; (631) 852–3232; www.suffolkcountyny.gov.

Features 287 acres where the Peconic River drains into Flanders Bay, campsites, fishing, and a 2.5-mile hiking trail.

Meschutt Beach County Park, Shinnecock Canal to Canal Road, Hampton Bays; (631) 852–8205, (631) 854–4949 (off-season); www.suffolkcountyny.gov.

One thousand feet on Peconic Bay near Shinnecock Canal.

New Suffolk Beach, First Street, off New Suffolk Avenue and Main Street, New Suffolk; (631) 765–5182.

Town of Southold beach with 200 feet on Peconic Bay.

Otis G. Pike Preserve and Peconic Headwaters Natural Resources Management Area, between Route 25A and the Long Island Expressway, Calverton; (631) 444–0273; www.dec.state.ny.us.

Has 4,500 acres of pine and oak forest, fields, wetlands, and small ponds. The Peconic River runs through the area. Good bird-watching, fishing, and canoeing. Unmarked roads and trails for hiking across the site. Hunters use this area October through March. Access by New York State Department of Environmental Conservation permit (free).

Robert Cushman Murphy County Park, off River Road at Swan Pont, Manorville; (631) 854–4949; www.co.suffolk.ny.us.

Features 2,200 acres in the Peconic River watershed, with fishing (license required) and a free boat ramp for canoes and electric-powered boats.

South Jamesport Beach, off Peconic Bay Boulevard, South Jamesport; (631) 727–5744.

Town of Riverhead beach with 3,000 feet on Peconic Bay.

Shelter Island Sound

Wades Beach, Shore Road, off West Neck Road; (631) 749–0291.

Town of Shelter Island beach with 500 yards on Shelter Island Sound.

Shinnecock Bay

Griffith Preserve, south on Quogue-Riverhead Road to Montauk Highway, go west for one-tenth of a mile, East Quogue; (631) 367–3225.

This seventeen-acre preserve is owned by the Nature Conservancy and is one of only two nature preserves along Shinnecock Bay. The preserve has one trail, about a third of a mile long, that leads through pine-oak woods and oak-hickory woodlands. Watch for poison ivy as you walk. Tidal salt marsh borders the preserve on the east.

Quogue Wildlife Refuge, off Old Country Road, Quogue; (631) 653–4771; www.quoguerefuge.com.

This 300-acre refuge has 7 miles of guided trails. For views of the Quantuck Bay estuary, take the Fairy Dell boardwalk at the south of the parking lot. Quantuck Bay connects Moriches and Shinnecock Bays.

Ruth Wales DuPont Sanctuary, at the end of Captain's Neck Lane, Southampton; (631) 329–7689.

This 31.5-acre preserve owned by the Nature Conservancy sits on Shinnecock Bay and is one of the most productive local shellfish and finfish bays. You can see horseshoe crabs, ribbed mussels, and fiddler crabs when the tide is out. Wear waterproof shoes and watch for poison ivy.

Smithtown Bay

Callahans Beach, end of Callahans Beach Road, off Route 25A, Fort Salonga; (631) 754–9808.

Town of Smithtown beach with 300 feet on Smithtown Bay, off Long Island Sound.

Long Beach, Long Beach Road, off Moriches Road, Nissequogue; (631) 584–9683.

Town of Smithtown beach with 300 feet on Smithtown Bay, off Long Island Sound.

Short Beach, off Boney Lane from Moriches and Long Beach Roads, Nissequogue; (631) 360–7654.

The oyster sloop *Christeen* at the Waterfront Center in Oyster Bay

Town of Smithtown beach with 300 feet on Smithtown Bay, off Long Island Sound.

Southold Bay

Crescent Beach, Shore Road, off West Neck Road, Shelter Island; (631) 749–0291.

Town of Shelter Island beach with 600 feet on Southold Bay, northwest side of Shelter Island.

Excursions

Bob's Canoe Rentals, P.O. Box 529, Kings Park 11754; (631) 269–9761; www.canoe rentalslongisland.com.

Season is mid-March through November. Location is the Nisse-quogue River between Kings Park and Smithtown; guided tours on request.

Christeen and ***Tahiti,*** 1 West End Avenue, Oyster Bay; (516) 922–SAIL; www.thewaterfront center.org.

The oyster sloop *Christeen* and the wooden ketch *Tahiti* are owned by the Waterfront Center. Sloop season is June to September. The *Tahiti* offers sunset sails around Oyster Bay, Cold Spring Harbor, and Long Island Sound, 7:00 P.M. Fridays in July and August; reservations required. The Waterfront Center is open 9:00 A.M. to 5:00 P.M. daily, Friday until dusk, May to October. It rents beginner kayaks and performance kayaks (with rudders).

A kayaker on the Nissequogue River in Smithtown

Connetquot River Canoe Rentals, Nicoll Bay, Oakdale; (631) 269–2774.

Rentals: thirty-six canoes, twenty-five kayaks, instruction. Trips: March to mid-November, 8:00 A.M. to 6:00 P.M. daily; book ahead. Six-boat minimum. Canoe area is a 3-mile section on the Connetquot River, Nicoll Bay to Sunrise Highway; round-trip about 3 hours. River forks near Sunrise; main fork to Bubbles Falls, other to Bayard Cutting Arboretum.

Dinghy Shop at South Bay Sailing Center, 334 South Bayview Avenue, Amityville; (631) 264–0005; www.dinghyshop.com.

Rentals, kayaks, sailboats, tours, instruction, and guided tours. Wednesday twilight paddling trips tours 6:00 P.M. to dusk all summer. Full-moon paddling trips. Season is April to November; call for winter hours.

Eagle's Neck Paddling Co., 49295 Main Road, Southold; (631) 765–3502; www.eagles neck.com.

Double and single kayak and canoe rentals, two hours to full day. Weekend, weekly, and one-to three-month lease rates. Wildlife, sunset, and full-moon tours.

Empire Kayaks, 4 Empire Boulevard, Island Park; (516) 889–8300; www.empirekayaks.com.

Sales, rentals, sunset paddles, full-moon paddles, yoga paddles, surf kayaking and kayak fishing, and instruction. Open year-round 9:00 A.M. to 6:00 P.M. weekdays, 8:00 A.M. to 6:00 P.M. weekends. Closed Tuesday.

***Explorer* tour boat at Atlantis Marine World,** 431 East Main Street, Riverhead; (631) 208–9200, ext. 106; www.atlantismarineworld.com.

Season is May to October. Group rates available. Two-hour environmental boat tour of the Peconic River and Flanders Bay is conducted by Cornell Cooperative Extension marine naturalists.

Glacier Bay Sports, 81-C Fort Salonga Road, Northport; (631) 262–9116; and 2979 Montauk Highway, Brookhaven; (631) 286–0567; www.glacierbay sports.com.

Company rents kayaks and offers tours and instruction. Tour sites include many Long Island waters, including Northport Harbor and the upper and lower Carmans River from Yaphank Lake to the Great South Bay.

Kayaken Outfitters, (516) 635–0997 or (631) 467–5163; www.kayaken-outfitters.com.

Kayak tours, indoor and outdoor lessons for individuals and groups. Call for details.

Lauren Kristy Paddlewheel Cruises, foot of Clinton Avenue, Bay Shore Marina, Bay Shore; (631) 321–0199; www.lauren kristy.com.

Season is April to November. Call for rates. Sightseeing on Great South Bay. Reservations required.

Matt-A-Mar Marina, 2255 Wickham Avenue, Mattituck; (631) 298–4739 or (631) 298–4739; www.mattamar.com.

Kayak rentals 9:00 A.M. to 4:00 P.M. daily, May to October.

Nissequogue River Canoe and Kayak Rentals, Nissequogue River, Smithtown; (631) 979–8244; www.canoerentals.com.

Rentals: fifty canoes and twenty-five kayaks. Trips, April to November daily, depending on weather and tide. Instructor available for extra fee. Tidal river flows north or south between Kings Park and Smithtown.

Peconic Paddler, 89 Peconic Avenue, Riverhead; (631) 369–9500; www.peconicpaddler.com.

Canoe and kayak rentals. Daily trips, 8:00 A.M. to 5:00 P.M. Open daily except Tuesday, late April to mid-October. Transport to Manorville for 8-mile paddle.

Personal Touch Kayak Lessons and Tours, (631) 691–2396; www.personaltouchkayaktours.com

Guided kayak tours and lessons at twenty-five locations in Nassau and Suffolk Counties. Group tours every weekend (schedule on Web site). Call for reservations. No unescorted rentals.

The Peconic River in Riverhead

Setauket Harbor Canoes & Kayaks, 30 Shore Road, Setauket Harbor, East Setauket; (631) 751–2706.

Kayak, canoe, and shell rentals. Daily and environmental awareness tours. Open 10:00 A.M. to 5:00 P.M. daily. Fee, from $30 per day; group rates, instruction.

Shelter Island Kayak Tours, Route 114 at Duvall Road, Shelter Island; (631) 749–1990; www.kayaksi.com.

Kayak rentals, tours, April to November.

Suffolk County Marine Environmental Learning Center, 3690 Cedar Beach Road, Southold; (631) 852–8660.

Kayaks, instructions, safety courses, and canoe tours of seventy-acre salt marsh. Season is May to October. Minimum six people; registration required.

Wetlands Discovery Cruises, Shore Road, off Main Street, Stony Brook; (631) 751–2244; www.wmho.org.

Runs May through October 31. Call for rates. Activities: ninety-minute cruises from Stony Brook Harbor into wetlands aboard a thirty-five-passenger pontoon boat, guided by a Stony Brook University naturalist. Educational group cruises available.

Exploring Cedar Beach Creek near the Suffolk County Marine Environmental Learning Center in Southold

CHAPTER 5

In Your Backyard

By Bryn Nelson

In the early morning sunshine, an Eastern gray squirrel scampers across a split-rail fence like a gymnast navigating a balance beam. An Eastern cottontail rabbit emerges less gracefully from a vegetable garden, sated and seeking a nap in a brush pile. Chickadees and cardinals congregate in an oak tree, while pseudoscorpions and millipedes stir within its fallen leaves below.

Usually unbidden, sometimes unwelcome, often unexpected, nature has followed us home.

As extensions of the natural world around us, Long Island's backyards host a remarkable diversity of life, whether a colony of Italian wall lizards playing hide-and-seek in a summer garden or a white-tailed deer standing statuesque in the winter snow. Under a blazing sun, worker honeybees dance on a box hive's honeycomb to communicate the direction of a prime nectar source, while female fireflies flash their coded messages in the moonlight to beckon potential mates—or potential meals.

Crows, fixtures of suburbia, amid garbage in East Norwich

The immediacy of life around our homes can pose dilemmas, but it also can create unique opportunities to observe the fauna that define Long Island. Some of these creatures are relative newcomers, while others are familiar standbys. Some may be seen in a new light, while others live unseen just beyond our suburban porch lights. But if our patience holds and our tolerance allows, all of them can teach us about the intricate roles of predator and

An Eastern gray squirrel at Sagamore Hill in Oyster Bay

A raccoon prowling at night in Oyster Bay

prey, about survival strategies that change with the seasons, and about the resilient nature of the creatures that have literally arrived at our doorsteps.

Determined observers have tallied thousands of different species within their own yards, a list dominated by a carnival of insects found fluttering or crawling or marching within feet of their backdoors. Thousands more are doubtless all around—miniature acrobats and weightlifters and beauties whose performances we can only imagine.

Mammalian visitors, whether deer or raccoon or squirrels or voles, often provide the clearest signs that nature's domain knows no bounds, to the delight of children or the dismay of gardeners. The enticing habitats around our homes—including tulip beds that offer sustenance to squirrels and garbage cans that delight raccoons—have reminded us again and again that we, too, are players in the environmental dramas unfolding all around us.

Among the newer arrivals various tales have sprung up to explain the emigration of a small group of grass-green wall lizards from the north of Italy to the heart of Long Island. No one knows for sure how many of the cold-blooded reptiles are now basking in the sunshine of suburbia, but they have adapted remarkably well to their adopted homeland. A sunny spot to provide warmth and aid their metabolism, a haven in the cracks and crevices of walls and gardens, a steady diet of crickets, spiders, and other small creatures—all are abundant.

As for spiders, scientists say the number of known species on the Island could easily top 600. Our orb-weaver spiders are perhaps best known for incorporating dozens of yards of silk into a sticky web that can span up to 2 feet, and for frightening the unfortunate arachnophobes who stumble into it. Others, like the stealthy

An Italian wall lizard at the Garden City Nursery School

wolf spider, hunt their prey on the ground. And still others disguise themselves on trees to resemble bark or lichens, or spin tiny webs within lingering piles of backyard leaves.

It is within the largely forgotten layers of decomposing leaf litter, sometimes called the "poor man's jungle," where scientists have documented the greatest diversity of life.

Among the teeming masses living in the litter, tiny mites graze on algae and fungi. Some beetles do the same. Other creatures such as centipedes and pseudoscorpions hunt the unwary, serving as Lilliputian lions and tigers.

A sowbug feasting on a rotting tree stump at Planting Fields Arboretum State Historic Park in Oyster Bay

Through successive layers of grazing and digesting, the progressively smaller organisms effectively process dead plants and animals into more manageable morsels. Bacteria and fungi eventually convert the smallest bits to the organic nutrients that enable the growth of new oaks and maples, hickories, and cherries.

As the street lamps flicker on and children reluctantly head inside, these backyard trees become the perfect backdrops for the evening performers—other denizens of the insect empire such as moths and leafhoppers, katydids, and cicadas.

And somewhere up above it all, as color fades and touch and sound begin to vie with sight for supremacy, a screech owl or great horned owl may have perched, the night watchman in the suburban drama of life and death on Long Island.

A young great horned owl in a nest at Bethpage State Park

In Cold Spring Harbor a cicada hanging on the underside of a rail fence

Eastern Gray Squirrel

What: Long Island's ubiquitous Eastern gray squirrel, *Sciurus carolinensis*, may commandeer our backyard bird feeders and do a number on our flower bulbs—though not daffodils and fritillaria, which make the squirrel ill. But a highly adaptable rodent that can race up to 20 mph; leap 6 feet in a single bound; and use its bushy tail like a rudder, umbrella, or parachute is nevertheless something to behold.

When: Since gray squirrels don't hibernate in the winter, their activities can be observed year-round. In fall the rodents stash hoarded acorns and other nuts in separate hiding places, and in winter they follow their keen sense of smell to reclaim most of them, sniffing them out even under a foot of snow. In late winter males begin chasing after females, and squirrel pups can arrive both in spring and fall.

Where: Squirrel antics are common wherever there are trees, especially oak, maple, and hickory.

Keep in Mind: Not all Eastern gray squirrels are in fact gray. Natural variations in hair color are common, and Long Island's scattered pockets of black squirrels are actually the result of an alternative pigmentation within the gray squirrel population, as are the much rarer white squirrels.

A squirrel with a mouthful on a Long Island utility line

Italian Wall Lizard

What: Long Island's only lizard species likely made its debut in the late 1960s when a batch of would-be pets escaped from a broken crate behind a pet store in Garden City. Since then the grass-green reptiles have adapted beautifully to the Island and multiplied by the thousands. Unlike other resident alien species, the lizards appear to have had little negative impact on the local flora and fauna, perhaps because Long Island previously lacked a native lizard species of its own. And unlike other reptiles the lizards are thriving in our landscaped yards and gardens, where meals of spiders and insects are plentiful, hiding places are abundant, and basking spots are as common as the nearest ornamental rock or railroad tie.

When: The lizards normally stay active from late March through October; late morning and late afternoon are best for viewing, since the lizards usually take cover during the hottest part of the day.

Where: "Ground L," as it's known, now includes a large swath of Garden City. Thanks to some human intervention, however, the lizards now occupy prime real estate from the Hamptons to the Bronx—and more than two dozen colonies in between. If you don't yet have lizards in your own yard, two of the best accessible viewing spots are the Garden City Bird Sanctuary on Tanners Pond Road and the Garden City Community Park on Cherry Valley Avenue.

Keep in Mind: Like other lizards, Italian wall lizards will release their tails to escape pursuers, whether cats or children. And although the harmless lizards have captivated many Long Island residents, your neighbors won't necessarily thank you for introducing them to your neighborhood.

The Italian wall lizard—by accident, Long Island's only lizard species

Little Critters in the Leaf Litter

What: A seemingly ordinary pile of leaves can host thousands of miniature creatures, including an impressive range of centipedes, millipedes, pseudoscorpions, springtails, spiders, mites, and other creepy-crawlies. This incredibly diverse "poor man's jungle," as some have called it, could be as close as your own backyard.

When: Life abounds from spring through fall, though you can likely find some movement beneath the insulating leaf layer in winter months as well. Tiny arthropods known as springtails may even appear on the snow on warmer winter days, where they look like little spots of dancing pepper.

Where: To begin exploring in your own yard, you'll need a way to sift out the larger leaves, twigs, and debris. Try condensing several handfuls of leaves through a tennis racket held over an open pillowcase. When you've accumulated a pound or so of filtered debris in the pillowcase, dump it out onto a white plastic tablecloth. Patience and a good magnifying glass can help you spot many of your yard's smallest inhabitants, and a good field guide can help you identify them. The American Museum of Natural History's guide "Life in the Leaf Litter" is available for free at http://research.amnh.org/biodiversity/center/publ/pubscbc.html#leaf.

Keep in Mind: Not every creature in the leaves is mild-mannered. Spiders can bite, millipedes have poisonous pincers, and centipedes use poison to defend themselves as well; so, be careful what you grab, or wear a good pair of gardening gloves.

A salamander on the underside of a mushroom, found in leaves in Oyster Bay

Nocturnal Insects

What: The flash of a firefly's mating beacon has become a hallmark of summer, though the other night owls of the insect world can offer memorable spectacles as well. Leaf hoppers, praying mantises, and an astounding array of colorful moths all have inspired "oohs and ahs" throughout Long Island.

When: Summer nights are obviously best, though early risers like grasshoppers, katydids, and crickets can start their music-making in the late afternoon and early evening.

Where: You can attract and spot many of these nighttime neighbors within your own backyard. One way is to hang a white bed sheet over a tree branch or clothesline along with an ultraviolet light. The light will attract the insects, which will perch on the sheet and allow you to inspect them. A digital camera and a good field guide can provide a fun way to pore over your virtual collection at your own pace.

Keep in Mind: Mosquitoes, the nocturnal insects we love to hate, sense warmth and exhaled carbon dioxide to locate their prey. Protective clothing and bug spray will keep them at bay, but remember that excessive spraying may repel other insects as well.

In East Norwich, a katydid, a creature of summer nights

White-tailed Deer

What: The Island's prolific, if sometimes problematic, resident deer abound throughout the eastern half of Long Island and are quickly spreading westward. Love them or hate them, the large mammals known as *Odocoileus virginianus* are among the most visible of the Island's fauna and remarkable for their athleticism, resourcefulness, and grace.

When: Anytime, though late afternoons are best for viewing. Fawns generally arrive in pairs by mid-spring, while bucks are in their prime during fall and early winter, before they lose their antlers.

Where: Apart from landscaped yards, you will likely encounter deer in any state or county park in the eastern two-thirds of Suffolk County. Some of the more scenic examples of varying deer habitats include Fire Island National Seashore, Connetquot River State Park Preserve in Oakdale, the Atlantic Double Dunes Preserve in East Hampton, and Mashomack Preserve on Shelter Island.

Keep in Mind: No matter what your position on deer overpopulation measures, please don't feed the deer. It's illegal in New York State. Drive carefully, especially during late fall and early winter breeding season, when distracted deer may jump onto roadways and give you an especially close view.

Deer on private property in North Haven, near Sag Harbor

Interview with a Vole

His face is furry and seemingly innocent, a surprise given that the meadow vole inspires fear in vegetables and tree roots everywhere. One recent day the vole, one of Long Island's major nuisances, paused at the opening of his grassy burrow and agreed to take questions about his life and times.

Q. You are, what, 3 inches long?

A. Four inches. We meadow voles are 3 to 5 inches, plus tail. Our tails can be 2 inches. There's another, less common Long Island vole—the pine vole—but it's smaller. Four inches, tops. And the tail is stubbier. Half an inch, maybe.

Q. I love your fur.

A. Thanks. I'm typical of a meadow vole—dark brown to black, and my fur is just a smidge coarse. I admit, the pine voles are striking. Soft brown fur, more of a chestnut color.

Q. But, you are rodents, correct?

A. Duh!

Q. And you live underground, down there in your deep, dark vole holes.

A. Sounds like you've been reading from the Web site of the New York State Integrated Pest Management Program again. Actually, we meadow voles live in shallow tunnels. We use our teeth to clip away a path in the vegetation—"runways," they're called. Pine voles often have tunnel networks less than a foot underground.

Q. Tell us about your family.

A. Two words: large and extended. Or, is that three words? We produce several litters per year, from March to November. Three voles per litter usually.

Q. Is it not also true that you sometimes eat your own young?

A. Sad but true.

Q. On Long Island it seems you live everywhere.

A. And you humans don't? We're at home on the sand dunes, on salt marshes, in the fruit orchards in the East End, pine woods, and in gardens from Manhasset to Montauk.

Chewing a bleak path of wanton botanical destruction, we eat the roots of fruit trees, tree bark, vegetables, shrubs, grains, seeds, and flowers. Hostas. Hostas just might be our favorite.

Q. There you have it. Fat and happy. The vole.

A. Hold on there. The life of a vole isn't one big picnic. That's only about 90 percent of the time. We also live in fear of evil predators—hawks, owls, red fox, snakes, and cats.

Q. That sounds very difficult.

A. It's not easy. And occasionally we have our humanitarian moments. Perhaps you've heard of the long-running study of terns on Great Gull Island.

Q. The American Museum of Natural History runs it.

A. Yes, and do you know how they created the open spaces where these endangered terns nest? In 1980 they reintroduced us voles to the island and we cleaned that place of most vegetation in less than a year. The museum says Great Gull now hosts the largest population of nesting roseate and common terns in the Western Hemisphere.

Q. Voles aren't endangered, are they?

A. Next question.

—JOE HABERSTROH

Life of a Rabbit

When it comes to perpetuating the species, rabbits are the Energizer bunnies of the animal world.

The female *Sylvilagus floridanus*, or Eastern cottontail, that resides on Long Island can start reproducing at the age of three months. She can give birth to three or four litters a year. Consider that each litter contains five or six baby bunnies—newborns are blind, deaf, and hairless—and that the female can breed again within hours. One pair of rabbits and their offspring could theoretically conceive five million young during a five-year period.

You don't need Elmer Fudd to keep the bunny brigades in check, however. What with disease, traffic, and predators such as foxes, owls, and hawks, about 85 percent of the cottontail population dies each year. Even though they can run 25 mph, hop more than 9 feet in the air, and run zigzags to evade predators, most rabbits don't usually make it past their second birthday.

Rabbits in the grass outside a Melville office

But while they're at large, these voracious vegetarians chow down on succulent grasses, tasty garden vegetables, and the tender green shoots of tulips. They graze all night—they're quite the gourmands—with 17,000 taste buds, compared with 10,000 in humans. In winter they nibble on the twigs, bark, and buds of oak, maple, dogwood, sumac, and birch trees. Their long incisors grow continuously and they have nearly 360-degree vision, although they can only see shades of gray. Contrary to popular belief they don't live in warrens. Cottontails—just one of at least fifty-three species of rabbits in the world—have a home range of five to eight acres and live in slight depressions in the ground or beneath a pile of brush, where they curl up and nap the day away.

Actually, Eastern cottontails spend most of their time alone. Baby rabbits stay in a grass- and fur-lined nest with their mother for about four weeks. By then mom is pregnant again and they're on their own to raid gardens, dodge predators, and perpetuate the species.

—IRENE VIRAG

Trivia of the Tiny

If they all survived over a five-month period, the descendants of one pair of houseflies would number 190 quintillion—enough for every human on the planet to be buzzed by a swarm of 30 billion flies. In reality scientists estimate that about 10 quintillion insects are living on the planet at any given time—still enough for a personal entourage of about 1.6 billion.

■ ■ ■

With some 350,000 named species, beetles account for the single largest order of animals on Earth.

■ ■ ■

An ant can lift and carry fifty times its own weight, the equivalent of a 125-pound woman carrying a Hummer SUV on her back.

■ ■ ■

A termite queen can live for fifty years or more, though some researchers suspect her life span may even reach the century mark.

■ ■ ■

One type of flea can long jump 150 times its own body length, the equivalent of a 4-foot, 10-inch sixth-grader vaulting the length of two football fields.

■ ■ ■

For high-jumping feats, though, nothing beats a common garden dweller known as a spittle bug. It can leap up to 115 times its own height, the equivalent of that same 4-foot, 10-inch sixth-grader hurdling a 556-foot-tall skyscraper.

■ ■ ■

The painted lady holds the butterfly record for long-distance migration: 4,000 miles, traveling from North Africa to Ireland.

■ ■ ■

A standard one-ounce letter weighs as much as one-hundred monarch butterflies.

■ ■ ■

Wasps feeding on fermented juice have been known to get drunk and pass out.

■ ■ ■

Houseflies search for sugar with their feet, which are ten million times more sensitive than the human tongue.

■ ■ ■

As the vector for the bacterial-borne bubonic plague, or Black Death, fleas killed twenty-five million Europeans in the fourteenth century.

■ ■ ■

Some butterflies can fly at altitudes of up to 20,000 feet.

■ ■ ■

A midge beats its wings 62,760 times every minute.

■ ■ ■

A female praying mantis sometimes bites off the head of her male companion during mating, but the male will continue mating while headless.

■ ■ ■

Scientists estimate that the male silk moth can detect a few hundred pheromone molecules among twenty-five quintillion molecules.

■ ■ ■

One kind of dragonfly has been clocked at 35 mph over short distances, making it the fastest known insect.

■ ■ ■

To produce one pound of honey, 10,000 bees must work their entire lives, collectively visiting two million flowers and flying 50,000 miles.

■ ■ ■

Aquatic whirligig beetles have divided compound eyes, allowing their upper eyes to see above the water surface while the lower eyes peer below it.

Life of a Pseudoscorpion

Resembling a pint-size scorpion or ghostly lobster in miniature, the pseudoscorpion lurks in Long Island's woodlands, prowls its intertidal zones, and haunts the musty bookshelves of its older suburban homes.

Although rarely noticed because of its sesame-seed-like size, the pale-bodied arthropod is nonetheless an important predator in the largely hidden world within a pile of decaying leaves, beneath a clump of shoreline debris, or between pieces of rotting tree bark. But it also hunts its prey between stacks of newspapers, beneath peeling wallpaper, or within the pages of aging novels. Where readers once feasted on the words of Hemingway and Hawthorne, the creature sometimes called a book scorpion finds its reward in a meal of book lice.

More closely related to spiders than to insects, the eight-legged pseudoscorpion can easily move forward, backward, or sideways. Its chief attributes, however, are its two pincerlike claws called pedipalps, both of which extend almost half the length of its body. The predator seizes its prey with its pedipalps, then subdues the unlucky louse, mite, springtail, or insect larva with poison secreted through ducts at the tips of its claws. A final death grip seals the poisoned prisoner's fate.

More than 2,500 species of pseudoscorpions are known throughout the world, including about 350 in North America. But the ubiquitous creatures are rarely considered nuisances since they feed on insect pests, lack a stinger like true scorpions, and pose no danger to humans.

During courtship the male with the largest pedipalps almost always wins a fight for a female, though an overly large endowment may impede him in other key activities such as traveling and catching prey. Mating begins with an elaborate dance, during which the male grasps the female by her pedipalps in an embrace of sorts. Half dragging her, the male positions his mate over one of his deposited sperm packets, which she takes up through her genital opening.

Before long the mother-to-be begins spinning silk through ducts in her jaws, gradually forming a brooding chamber attached to her abdomen. Within it she may lay up to several dozen eggs. Adults endure winters within the safety of silken cocoons as well, perhaps a main reason why they can survive for two to three years.

But don't call them homebodies. Although they lack wings, pseudoscorpions rely on an unusual form of hitchhiking known as phoresy. Using their claws, the creatures cling to the legs of beetles, flies, or wasps—and sometimes birds or mammals—essentially grabbing a free ride to a new home.

—BRYN NELSON

MUSEUMS AND
EDUCATIONAL CENTERS

By Laura Mann

Along with its many outdoor gems, Long Island boasts several collections devoted to the natural world. Here is a selection.

Cold Spring Harbor Fish Hatchery and Aquarium, Route 25A, Cold Spring Harbor; (516) 692–6768; www.cshfha.org.

Opened in 1883, the hatchery became a nonprofit educational facility in 1982. View all ages of brook, brown, and rainbow trout. Also: freshwater fish, turtles, and amphibians native to New York.

Cold Spring Harbor Whaling Museum, Main Street and Route 25A, Cold Spring Harbor; (631) 367–3418; www.csh whalingmuseum.org.

Picturesque four-room museum displays memorabilia such as a rare nineteenth-century 30-foot whaleboat, harpoons, scrimshaw, and a diorama of the whaling port in its 1850 heyday. Educational programs emphasize current and historical whaling practices, whale biology, and conservation. Hear the song of a humpback whale and try a hands-on activity.

Cornell Cooperative Extension of Nassau County, 239 Fulton Avenue, Hempstead; (516) 292–7990; www.cce .cornell.edu/~nassau.

An educational not-for-profit association offering programs and research-based information on

A child and her South American wood turtle at the Cold Spring Harbor Fish Hatchery and Aquarium's turtle pageant

horticulture, environmental issues, food and nutrition, consumer issues, parenting, 4-H youth development, and outdoor educational camping programs. Call for schedules.

East End Seaport Museum, Third Street and ferry dock, Greenport; (631) 477–2100; www.eastendseaport.org.

Exhibits include saltwater aquariums, rare lighthouse lenses, and World War II artifacts. Also, educational cruises, lectures, and a September maritime festival.

Garvies Point Museum and Preserve, 50 Barry Drive, Glen Cove; (516) 571–8010; www.co.nassau.ny.us/parkmuse .html.

Part of a sixty-two-acre preserve overlooking Hempstead Harbor, this county-run museum focuses on local geology, the earliest inhabitants, and archaeology. There are 5 miles of trails and a self-guided nature trail.

Hicksville Gregory Museum, Heitz Place and Bay Avenue, Hicksville; (516) 822–7505; www.gregorymuseum.org.

The museum holds Long Island's largest rock and mineral collection, 5,000 butterfly and moth specimens, shells, fossils, and dinosaur artifacts.

Long Island Maritime Museum, 86 West Avenue, West Sayville; (631) 854–4974; www.limaritime.org.

Features the history of Long Island fishing, the Great South Bay oyster industry, and boating. See restored oyster vessels, sailboats, oyster shacks, a preserved bayman's cottage, exhibits on the U.S. Life Saving Service, and the 1888 sailing dredge boat *Priscilla*.

Museum of Long Island Natural Sciences, Earth and Space Sciences Building, Center Drive, Stony Brook University, Stony Brook; (631) 632–8230; http://pbisotopes.ess.sunysb.edu/molins.

Exhibits in the Earth and Space Sciences Building tell the relationship of humans and nature on Long Island, especially involving the sea. Dioramas, changing exhibits, nature walks, lectures, stargazing evenings.

Science Museum of Long Island, 1526 North Plandome Road, Manhasset; (516) 627–9400; www.smli.org.

Open daily; call for program schedules. Fees vary. Science activity center at Leeds Pond Preserve, with thirty-six acres of woods and beachfront. Offers field and lab studies, organic gardens, animals, educational programs, summer day camp, off-site fossil digs, nature walks, and travel programs.

South Shore Nature Center, off Bayview Avenue, East Islip; (631) 224–5436.

Has 206 acres, 2.3-mile self-guided trail through salt marsh; upland oak and hickory forest, indoor honeybee hive, nature

museum (with saltwater fish tank and reptiles), picnic area and butterfly garden, and weekend family programs.

Suffolk County Marine Environmental Learning Center, 3690 Cedar Beach Road, Southold; (631) 852–8660; www.cce.cornell.edu/suffolk/MARprograms/SCMELC.htm.

Run by the Cornell Cooperative Extension of Suffolk County, this educational center offers instruction and outreach programs on environmental issues, marine biology, aquaculture, fishing, salt marsh ecology, wildlife rehabilitation, birding, and salt marsh ecology. Group tours available.

Suffolk County Vanderbilt Museum and Planetarium, 180 Little Neck Road, Centerport; (631) 854–5555; www.vanderbiltmuseum.org.

Former home of William K. Vanderbilt II features a Hall of Fishes with 2,000 marine specimens and a wing with vertebrate and invertebrate specimens.

An inhabitant of the butterfly and moth vivarium at the Sweetbriar Nature Center in Smithtown

Planetarium shows explore the heavens in its 60-foot domed Sky Theater. Children's programs.

Sweetbriar Nature Center, 62 Eckernkamp Drive, Smithtown; (631) 979–6344; www.sweetbriarnc.org.

Has fifty-four acres; hiking trails through an array of habitats including wetlands, fields, and forests with views of the Nissequogue River; self-guided nature trails; butterfly and moth house (fee, open 10 A.M. to 4 P.M. daily, June-October); picnic area; and restrooms.

A sea urchin in the touch tank at the Suffolk County Marine Environmental Learning Center in Southold

Tackapausha Museum, Washington Avenue, Seaford; (516) 571–7443; www.co.nassau.ny.us/park muse.html.

Located in the eighty-acre Tacka-pausha Preserve, the museum has seasonal exhibits of local wildlife and plants to explain life sciences. Five miles of nature trails, nocturnal animal exhibit, educational programs including live fruit bats.

Theodore Roosevelt Nature Center, Jones Beach State Park, Ocean Parkway, exit at West End, Wantagh; (516) 679–7254; http://nysparks.state.ny.us.

Exhibits include a variety of marine habitats, including the South Shore Estuary Reserve, the seashore, and the dune environments. Stroll the environmental boardwalk or through the butterfly garden. Children will enjoy a special activity area. Call for schedule.

Theodore Roosevelt Sanctuary and Audubon Center, 134 Cove Road, Oyster Bay; (516) 922–3200; http://ny.audubon.org/trsac .htm.

This wildlife sanctuary and an environmental education center offer programs on birds, ponds, beaches, and other areas of natural history. The museum focuses on the history of American conservation and the accomplishments of Theodore Roosevelt, the "conservation president."

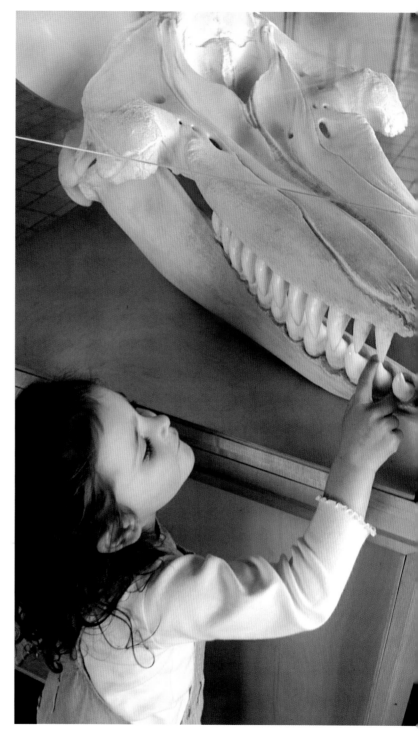

Checking teeth on the skull of a killer whale at the Theodore Roosevelt Nature Center at Jones Beach

INDEX

Page numbers in *italics* indicate photographs.

ABOUT THE *NEWSDAY* TEAM

Newsday's "Natural World" team at West Hills Park in Huntington: from left, photographer Bill Davis, garden columnist Irene Virag, science writer Bryn Nelson, Long Island reporter Jennifer Smith, and waters reporter Joe Haberstroh

Staff for *Newsday's Guide to Long Island's Natural World* includes executive editor Phyllis Singer; editor Harvey Aronson; news editor Lawrence Striegel; lead writers Joe Haberstroh, Bryn Nelson, Jennifer Smith, and Irene Virag; photographer Bill Davis; photo editor John Paraskevas; map designer Richard Cornett; photo technician Andreas Constantinou; researcher Laura Mann; chapter 2 tree illustrator Janet Hamlin; and writers Hugh McGuinness and Julie Claire Diop.

Photo Credits

All photos by *Newsday* photographer Bill Davis, with the exception of the following: p. 5, U.S. Fish and Wildlife Service; pp. 6 and 122, John H. Cornell Jr. of *Newsday*; pp. 25 top and 113 top, Joseph D. Sullivan; pp. 26, 31 top, 36 bottom, 76 bottom, 78, 83, 88, 95, 97, 99, 101, and 103, Ken Spencer of *Newsday*; pp. 36 top and 108, Kathy Kmonicek of *Newsday*; p. 37, John Paraskevas of *Newsday*; pp. 44 and 50 bottom, Karen Wiles Stabile of *Newsday*; pp. 45 top, 47, 49, 52, and 130, Michael E. Ach of *Newsday*; pp. 48 and 107 bottom, J. Michael Dombroski of *Newsday*; pp. 54, 79, and 96, Thomas A. Ferrara of *Newsday*; p. 55, John Griffin; p. 56, Randy Randazzo; pp. 58 and 134, Jim Peppler of *Newsday*; p. 59 bottom, Dick Kraus of *Newsday*; pp. 64 and 84, Richard Slattery; p. 70, Doug Kuntz; p. 75, Mia Aigotti of *Newsday*; pp. 81, 107 top, and 129 top, David L. Pokress of *Newsday*; p. 82, Maxine Hicks; pp. 85 and 112, Alejandra Villa of *Newsday*; p. 91 top and bottom, Rory McNish, Cornell Cooperative Extension of Suffolk County; p. 102, Don Jacobsen of *Newsday*; p. 104, Richard Harbus; p. 106, Daniel Goodrich of *Newsday*; p. 109 top, Dick Yarwood of *Newsday*; p. 111, Audrey C. Tiernan of *Newsday*; and p. 128, Patrick Oehler.